THE EVERGREEN REVOLUTION

DITCH FEAST OR FAMINE & SIGN COACHING
CLIENTS EVERY WEEK

ROSE RADFORD

authors
AND CO.

CONTENTS

PREFACE

While still in my twenties, I took home more in a year than my old bosses three ranks up. I achieved this using the Evergreen Revolution, while doing work that makes a real difference to people's lives. It works, and it will work for you.

Not long before that though, my business felt like a massive roller coaster of finances and emotions. I'd never worked so hard and earned so little. I knew something had to change... but what?

Over the next six months, I went from *just* breaking even to achieving profitable $60K-100K cash months and making $32 for every $1 spent. In that time period, I served hundreds of clients in life-changing coaching programs.

But, unlike everyone else, I didn't exhaust myself with big launches and creating a new offer every month. In fact, I didn't even write a sales page until we had crossed $400K in sales. Instead, I was able to do one thing really well: I used evergreen marketing systems to predictably sign clients every week.

This book reveals the details of how I did this and how evergreen marketing has also revolutionised countless clients' businesses.

You can discover:

- How to sign one, two, three or even more clients a week into your group coaching program.
- How to run a group coaching program with open enrolment.
- How to blend intimacy and automation to make more sales.
- How to grow your audience of future buyers.
- How to unblock your mindset towards money so you can receive more than ever before.

Instead of relying on exhausting launches, you could repeatedly create launch-sized revenue every month with evergreen marketing. If you're serious about building an online coaching business in order to help a lot of people and to give you a freedom-based lifestyle that provides for you and your family, the Evergreen Revolution is for you.

FREE RESOURCES

Do you like super valuable free stuff? Great! Here's how you can grab an insane bundle of digital resources to help you grow your business on evergreen – completely *free*.

The Inside Scoop on My Million-Dollar Evergreen Funnel

Inside this instant-access digital bundle, you'll receive:

- Our high-converting landing pages and an explanation of why they convert far above industry standard, including plug-and-play templates you can use right away.
- The two emails that generate the most applications to work with us in the entire funnel.
- Guidance on the simplest tech set-up that costs less than $150 a month.
- The three game-changing tweaks we made to our Facebook Ads to 10x our conversion rate and overall profit.

- Your own profit calculator for your evergreen funnel.

Download the bundle here: www.million-dollar-funnel.com

DEDICATION

For you, my valued reader and friend. I hope this book serves as the injection of inspiration, the kick in the behind and the boost of confidence you may need to go after your big business and life goals.

ACKNOWLEDGEMENTS

Shout out to all the incredible humans who helped me on this book journey, whether they realised they were helping or not.

Thank you to my publishing team for your support in getting all my content, ideas and thoughts into a book that readers can benefit from. It's a weird old process, this book-writing thing. I've swung violently between "this is utter rubbish" to "I'm a legit creative genius" repeatedly over the last few months. I'm proud of what we've managed to bring together.

To my incredible online community and amazing clients, you give me a huge sense of purpose in being able to walk alongside you and support you to become your most wildly successful selves.

I'm hugely grateful to my team who make running a business an absolute joy: Abi, Katie, Sammy, Tiesta, Lucy and everyone else who's been part of my internal or external team over the years.

While waiting for the coffee machine to spurt out a fresh brew one morning, I realised how grateful I was to my mum for giving me a crack at being on this planet for a while. Dad, I know you were involved too, but I think Mum made the lion's share of the effort on that specific front. Thank you, Mum *and*

Dad for always helping me be brave, believe in myself and never doubt my crazy ideas.

Finally, to my Ride or Die husband, Scott Radford. Doing this life with you is extraordinary. You weren't much use with this book but I figured you'd appreciate the heartfelt shout-out.

INTRODUCTION

I never imagined I'd write a book about the life-changing powers of selling and delivering a group coaching program using an evergreen model. It sounds as dry as a camel's sandal. But here we are.

This book will be far more valuable to you than a camel's sandal if you're running a coaching business that feels like it's constant hard work for minimal reward. Perhaps your sales are unpredictable and you struggle to see a clear path to where you can make both the impact and money you want without risking burnout.

Maybe you started coaching in the last year or two, and you're looking for information on how best to grow your fledgling venture into a fully grown business that gives you the freedom and meaningful work you left your last job to pursue.

Either way, you feel overwhelmed with all the things you could be doing to grow your business, so you find yourself jumping from one strategy to another, doubting your decision when you try to commit to one approach to grow your business. You offer a confusing range of offers with no real sales strategy behind them and you're not entirely sure where to focus your time and energy to get the biggest results.

You desire the ability to earn six figures a year or even six figures a month with consistent, predictable revenue that doesn't cause a bungee jump of emotions every month. You want the time and headspace to be more present for your clients and family without feeling like the business is going to fall away if you step out of it for more than a day. You want to know exactly who to serve and what to sell to them, and to create results your clients rave about. Most importantly, you need to know how to articulate the value of your life-changing work so you can be paid well in return.

One thing you're damn certain about is that you're here to be a wild success. You know even the sky isn't the limit and you're the kind of person who goes all in to make something happen when you want it enough. You know you're meant for more than what you're currently experiencing, and it frustrates the heck out of you that you can see what's possible but can't feel or taste it – yet.

I felt the same not too long ago and found myself stalking all the big names in the industry, trying to understand their path to success so I could reverse engineer it for myself. I would rewrite my messaging every two weeks. My continually updated Instagram bio reflected my perpetual confusion.

I was trapped between imposter syndrome, perfectionism and the firm belief that I was going to make a success of my business, even if it took ten years or more. I know what it feels like to see the end vision you desire but have no real clue how to get there.

In March 2020, when the pandemic caused global lockdowns, large companies pulled their marketing spend and most consumers' wallets closed up like Venus fly traps. I didn't know it at the time and the angels certainly didn't come down from heaven that day to sing me a celebratory song, but one decision I made at that time has snowballed into something I never dreamed of. Choosing to start and scale my Freedom Accelerator program has been one of the most life-defining choices I've ever made.

My business has allowed me to go from just breaking even every month to generating more than $50,000 in profit a month. Most importantly, it allows me to help other women create wild success for themselves too.

The graduates of Freedom Accelerator have retired husbands from jobs that no longer lit them up, moved to their dream countries, put their children into private schooling, hired help at home and invested in their personal well-being like never before, all as a direct result of their business success.

Whatever your unique version of success looks like, it's possible with a scalable business that works *for* you and your clients, rather than sucking the life out of you.

Much like you, I want to spend my life doing work that actually matters. You want to help people using what you know. You want to be paid good money for the value you bring to others, and you want to have the freedom of choice that running your own business can give. Working for someone else isn't going to cut it for you. In fact, you may have concluded that you make a terrible employee or will forever need to be an entrepreneur.

If that's you, you're in the right place.

This book is based on my trusted Freedom Accelerator program which teaches women coaches, consultants and experts how to craft, sell and scale a group coaching program on evergreen, without needing to launch every few months. If you're new to the word 'evergreen', it is a word from the world of marketing to mean the opposite of launching. When your programs are evergreen, they're open all year round. A good evergreen marketing system will result in you signing one to three, and sometimes more, new clients a week. I'll reveal how you can do that in this book.

I generated over a million pounds in cash into my business before I turned thirty. I created the financial resources to move my husband and me to our dream country, pay for a fairy tale wedding up front, put a large lump sum into a retirement fund, as well as remove the worry about the prices on a menu or how much it costs to do my favourite thing: travel the world.

The life of freedom, joy and meaningful impact that I've built in a short space of time blows my mind and it's all down to growing my business on evergreen.

There's no way I'm keeping this to myself. It's too bloody good to keep to myself. I want you to feel this level of personal success, financial overflow and pure joy in your work and life.

Why do I work specifically with women entrepreneurs? My work is all about putting more money in the hands of women through entrepreneurship.

The income gap between male and female entrepreneurs is bigger than the gender corporate salary gap. In the USA, employed women on average are paid around 18% less than men. The entrepreneurial income gap is 10% *higher* at around 28%. In other words, we women are doing it to ourselves. We make less money and pay ourselves less, even within the same industry.

This has to stop. And I believe we can make a massive shift towards gender income parity within entrepreneurship in my lifetime, and yours. I'm on a mission to help one thousand women become self-made millionaires by 2030. This book is part of that mission and a part of my body of work. I truly hope this book does you justice by inspiring in you a thought, an idea or even a massive shift towards your most free and successful self.

What version of wild success is calling you? What could you create in your life and for your family with an evergreen group coaching program as your vehicle for that success?

You're about to start on a journey of learning to create anything you want with an impactful business at the core of it. Don't hold back on those wild ideas, because whatever you want, wants you back.

PART 1

THE TRAP

1

THE COACHING BUSINESS TRAP

IT'S hard to know where your business is going when you're in unfamiliar territory. If you've been to Lisbon, you will know that the city is full of narrow, winding streets with steep slopes and cobblestones that trip you up if you're not looking carefully. It's easy to get lost in the maze of colourful houses and beautiful murals.

When my husband and I first moved to Lisbon, we lived in Alfama, which is the historic part of the city originally built by the Moors. The Moors built the streets this way as a form of defence so that any invading army that landed on the riverside would need to navigate the streets full of dead ends and unexpected twists and turns without getting lost, which is impossible if you are unfamiliar with the area.

For the first few weeks in Alfama, I repeatedly found myself lost while navigating our new neighbourhood. Even though I had a map on my phone, I kept overshooting and missing turns. The streets are so small that it's difficult to be certain where you are, and if your phone signal isn't great, the little blue circle on the map can't always keep up either. I was like an excited but timid toddler on the streets.

After a few weeks, I found myself navigating the streets of Alfama like a snakes and ladders game in which I knew how to find all the ladders and dodge all the snakes.

Just as I had been looking to my app as my source of truth rather than looking up and around me, I had been looking outside of myself at the way the online coaching industry currently operates as the most important source of truth. I had seemingly dismissed all the knowledge I'd gained while working as a strategy consultant at McKinsey & Company about how businesses outside the online space operate effectively, and I had trusted the online industry's approach to business over my own discernment.

I see this happen again and again for coaches and online entrepreneurs who decide that all their previous career and life experiences are irrelevant when it comes to serving clients and finding their place in a new market. They focus on not falling over their feet while walking on trip-hazard-filled cobblestone streets, trusting the wisdom of a map to navigate their journey rather than their own wisdom.

If I had known this sooner, I would have questioned far earlier in my business journey the industry's reliance on launches as the main way to make sales, rather than waiting over three years for the penny to finally drop.

This brings me to introduce you to the person I like to call the Roller Coaster Coach.

The Roller Coaster Coach Reality

The Roller Coaster Coach is doing pretty well; her clients get results and she's beginning to see momentum in her business in the form of $5,000 and $10,000 months, or even $20,000 and $50,000 months if she's launching.

Now she wants to scale past the six-figure revenue mark to multi-six figures, and maybe even to seven figures one day, and help a lot of people in the process.

But she uses high-pressure launches as her main way to make sales, and it's exhausting for her. Not only does her marketing suck the life out of her every few months, but she's turning clients away between launches and using a waitlist for her coaching programs instead. Right before it's time to launch again, she worries she's not serving her clients enough because she also needs to focus on planning her next launch.

As a result, she experiences really inconsistent sales, which makes her feel unsafe in her business. Although she's not afraid to put in the work, the Roller Coaster Coach is beginning to feel tired and frankly, underpaid.

But she's not one for giving up, and she chooses to keep going because she has goals to help a lot of people with her expertise. So what does she do in an attempt to make more money without so much hard work and time invested? She launches more offers.

In between her current launches, she creates more offers like courses and digital products in the hope they will give her more sales, but she learns that these courses don't necessarily sell themselves.

In fact, she soon learns that if she really wants to sell a lot of different coaching programs, she's got to have a specific marketing plan behind each of them. She made a couple of sales of her new program from her warm online audience to begin with, but if she really wants to serve a lot of clients with that program, she's going to have to get serious about a longer-term marketing strategy.

The only time this isn't true is when a coach already has a large, established social media following who regularly buy from her, but like most coaches, the Roller Coaster Coach is a good few years away from having that.

She also realises that she can't scale her group program because she would be overwhelmed with more than fifteen or twenty clients in it. Frankly, if she had fifty new clients in her group coaching program, she would feel like she had fifty new one-to-one clients, which would be overwhelming and far from fun.

The Roller Coaster Coach works hard to sell and deliver multiple offers through launches and ends up stuck at her current income level. What she really wants is a simple pathway to a profitable multi-six-figure or seven-figure business that only requires three to five hours a day to run.

Maybe you realise you are the Roller Coaster Coach. Or maybe you see other coaches being the Roller Coaster Coach and you want to avoid that ride entirely.

If that's the case, this book is exactly what you need. The good news is that we're about to fix all of that. If you don't implement what I'm about to reveal to you, you're going to experience the same problems, which I really, really don't want for you. I've been there and got the t-shirt. That particular t-shirt, however, I put in the charity shop pile rather than my suitcase when I moved to Lisbon.

My goal is to give you a simple path to multi-six or seven figures with one core offer and a simple launch-free marketing strategy to make it happen, so you can predictably sign clients into your program every week. If you've heard of evergreen marketing but wondered what it involves and whether it will work for you, you're definitely in the right place.

What Got You Here, Won't Get You There

To understand why so many coaches find themselves on this roller coaster and to help you avoid the same, we first need to look at the beliefs that have led them there.

The Roller Coaster Coach believes that launching is the best way to grow a coaching business; whether she believes this consciously or unconsciously, this belief has led to her focus on launching. This has to be one of the biggest myths in the online coaching industry. It's easy to understand why she thinks this, though. She sees coaches creating wildly successful launches, so she naturally believes that she also needs bigger and better launches.

You always know when an online entrepreneur is launching, because a launch is so in your face. The visibility of their launch triggers your confirmation bias and encourages you to believe that you must launch to make sales.

As a high achiever, the Roller Coaster Coach wants to follow the best in the industry and wants to use the best strategies to grow her business, but let me ask you... is launching really the best way to grow your business sustainably? It is worth asking whether the top companies in the world launch products over and over. We know that Fortune 500 companies *don't* use launching to make sales.

What happens when you focus on launching as your main source of sales in your coaching business is a series of unpredictable feast and famine cash cycles. Wait until you discover the cash received figures in my business in 2020 as a result of launching. It's a shocker.

The Roller Coaster Coach's audience becomes numb to all the launch promotion she's doing, and she is exhausted from creating all the marketing assets required for a launch every few months. The webinar slides, the landing pages, the forty-email sequences and dozens of social media posts. Only to shelve it all in her Google Drive and barely use it again.

This is not a business. It's a nightmare.

But an evergreen approach is like a secret back door for sales. You don't have to dance around the internet like a magic pony to make sales (reason 3,684,702 why I love evergreen marketing over launches).

Great businesses build assets that generate income over a number of years. Your assets include your marketing assets and your coaching programs. If you invest time and money into building those assets only to shelve them rather than continue to generate income from them (as is the case for many coaches relying on launches) you're leaving thousands, if not millions of dollars on the table.

You hurt your ability to grow your business sustainably if you continue to lead with launching as your main marketing strategy.

The second big belief the Roller Coaster Coach has, consciously or unconsciously, is that she has to run a group coaching program in cohorts, where everyone starts and stops at the same time. She sees other coaches run group programs in cohorts, so she naturally thinks that the cohort approach is what she needs to do, too.

She believes that's the best way to run a group coaching program because that's what school was like, but she hasn't questioned whether cohorts are the best way to serve her clients.

But is the school system really the best way to serve and support thirty students in one classroom? Within any group of people there are hares and there are tortoises. Your hares are the clients who want to jump ahead to month two in the program when they're only on week one. The tortoises take a little longer to integrate their learning and make progress. But the traditional school system forces an entire group of students to complete the curriculum at the same speed.

If you're serving people in a cohort-style program, you don't serve the hares effectively and they feel their progress is being held back. When the tortoises feel left behind in the group, they tell themselves that they're too behind, so they disengage and they don't get the big results they could have had.

So a cohort group coaching program doesn't actually serve people well.

Your process with a client does not need to depend on what other clients are doing. The success of a client is not based on what other clients are doing. I've learnt this to be true from running two different group coaching programs and discovering that it can really hurt your client experience to use cohorts. The reliance on launching along with cohort-based coaching programs are two sides of the same coin.

Can you use evergreen marketing *and* launches to make sales?

Yes, you can, but in my experience, for this to truly work, you need to use an "evergreen first" marketing strategy, rather than leading with launches and then trying to make sales outside of launch campaigns in an attempt to call that "evergreen".

I recommend honing your evergreen marketing strategy and having that on lock so you make sales all year round, and then launching a few times a year on top of that to add some creativity, fun and pizzazz into the mix.

Running a business that relies on making the bulk of your revenue by launching is dangerously unpredictable. But running launches to make extra money and to reach more people without the pressure to make all your revenue for the next three months in a two-week period is ideal. To be clear, I do not advocate for evergreen marketing from a place of hating launches and having been burned by them. I teach from a place of having loved creating profitable launches *and* having loved selling on evergreen, but finding that evergreen wins hands down every time, for so many reasons.

The Fully Booked One-to-One Coach

Maybe you're not the Roller Coaster Coach right now and instead, you're fully booked in your one-to-one coaching services and in desperate need of some time leverage through a group offer so you can serve more people, make more money, and get off the road to burn out that you're currently skipping along merrily.

Given that you've never coached your clients in a group setting before, you doubt whether clients will get good enough results in a group versus your one-to-one. You're not alone. I've found that most coaches initially believe their clients get better results working with them individually than in a group coaching program. But this simply isn't the case.

I can see why you might think that. As a coach, you naturally believe that you are the one who helps clients get results. But that's like saying your clients will only get results if you're there for them personally. Not only is that not the case, it's also a disempowering way to lead clients.

Have you ever stopped to question whether clients really do need one-to-one hand-holding to create results? Instead of relying on one-to-one calls to create transformations with clients, it's entirely possible to create a group coaching environment that delivers the same and even better results than working with you privately.

The biggest difference is in allowing your clients to leverage the power of the community. When clients work with you individually, their learning is limited to just you. When they work with you inside a curated group, their learning and transformation are accelerated by being in that community. By structuring the curriculum and the group calls effectively, you can provide a container for the biggest of transformations. Poorly crafted group coaching programs leave clients feeling deflated by their experience.

When you craft your curriculum with client results in mind, and learn how to run great group coaching calls where everyone feels seen, supported and heard, your group container can become even more valuable than a one-to-one experience with you. A small number of clients may be better off working with you individually. However, the vast majority actually benefit far more from being inside a group program with a community element.

For some types of sensitive coaching niches, you might feel that your clients don't want to be in a group situation because they're worried about having to share things that feel very personal and even shameful for them. I totally understand that; I've worked with clients who coach on things like binge and emotional eating and there's a lot of shame associated with those sorts of challenges.

But here's the thing: when you're in a community with others and you share something that feels shameful, or very personal, something that you may have hidden for a while, you actually have the opportunity to release that shame as you share it, as long as you are in a very safe, non-judgmental, supportive and secure community. This is exactly what you want to be creating inside your group coaching programs.

When you give people the space to share what feels hard to share, you give them the opportunity to transmute the negative feelings and transform them so much faster than they would by trying to figure it out on their own.

The Yellow Brick Road to Passive Income

Instead of offering a group coaching program, maybe you've considered selling passive, self-serve courses as it appears to be the easiest way to create more income and serve more people without you working more hours.

If that was really true, every course creator would be a six-figure course earner, and we know that's not the case. If you've ever tried to sell a course consistently and have a comparatively small audience, you'll have discovered that courses don't exactly sell themselves. Making a few sales of your $500 course every month might be fun but it is unlikely to get you to six figures any time soon.

Just because courses are usually cheap compared to your one-to-one, it doesn't make them easier to sell. People buy because they see value, not because something is cheap. In fact, the only thing that should be bought because it's cheap is an Easter egg the day after Easter. (For the non-Europeans, an Easter egg is a huge hollow egg made of chocolate filled with your favourite candy or sweets – the easiest way to my husband's heart.)

The maths on this will hurt, because to hit six figures with a $500 course, you need to find two hundred customers. Given a typical email list conversion rate is around 1%, you need about twenty thousand people on your email list to hit that figure. On the yellow brick road to the Land of Passive Income, that's a lot of lions and tin men you're going to need to meet.

Personally, I don't see the point in adding a new revenue stream unless it can reasonably generate at least $100,000 a year. Otherwise, you open yourself up to a whole lot of work for not much return after you've paid your transaction fees, tax and operational costs for selling that offer.

The alternative is to sell a group coaching program that commands a higher fee because it's more than just a self-serve course. Assuming your group coaching program is priced at $10,000, you only need to find ten new people to create the same amount of income as two hundred sales of a $500 course. Which is easier: finding ten people who will pay $10,000 or finding two hundred new customers?

If you can't play the "I have a huge online audience" card, then play the higher ticket card instead.

Whether you're the Roller Coaster Coach or the Fully Booked One-to-One Coach, this book will show you how to grow a group coaching program on evergreen without lots of launching or one-to-one time. You're in the right place.

2

L.E.A.P. INTO YOUR SEVEN-FIGURE BUSINESS MODEL

MANY LEADING seven and eight-figure online entrepreneurs and coaches do not use launching as a main driver of sales.

Instead, they have an evergreen marketing strategy which allows them to sign new clients every single week. Most of them have a scalable high-ticket group offer that sells year-round. These offers are seven-figure revenue streams for them.

You do not need to be a seven-figure earner to start thinking like one right now.

The Roller Coaster and Fully Booked One-to-One Coaches both want certainty and consistency in their income, and they want to have a huge impact on the world and help a lot of people, and be known and trusted in their space. One thing's for sure, having a high-value group coaching program is a really good way of making a name for yourself in your space.

When you show up for your clients, you want to do so in a big way. You do not want to be worried about sales and cash coming in. Your clients do not want to work with a financially stressed coach.

You also want to feel abundantly paid for the value and expertise you bring to your clients.

This is exactly what the CEO Coach has.

The CEO coach does what leading coaches do: she designs highly valuable premium offers that create epic client results; she implements a stable evergreen marketing model and experiences consistent cash months; she can create more income and impact while often working fewer hours than her peers.

She gets into the driving seat of her business.

To make this happen she focuses on a small number of specific things, each of which solves a different part of her overall problem. She implements the L.E.A.P. Method.

I have worked with hundreds of coaches to help them grow their businesses, and I've found they often struggle with the "Troublesome Trifecta".

The Troublesome Trifecta

1. Swapping Your Life for Cash
2. Scarily Unpredictable Income
3. Tumbleweed Instead of Leads

This trifecta of problems keeps coaches stuck and operating far below their income potential. It leaves them burnt out and disillusioned with their own businesses and the huge investment they've made into it, without the return they were hoping for.

Avoid these three core problems at all costs and you'll be able to build a business that stands the test of time and actually brings you freedom.

Swapping Your Life For Cash

You're experiencing the first problem if you spend so much time on Zoom that you sometimes miss the chance to have lunch until three in the afternoon. No matter how much time you spend serving clients on Zoom, you still feel like you are underpaid at the end of the tax year.

This is because you're either stuck trading time for money by only serving private clients or you're in Low Ticket Land with your prices – or both. The solution is to bring genuine time leverage into your business by serving more than one person at a time on a call.

When I made the shift from private coaching to a group coaching program, I went from serving five clients a week in five hours of Zoom to serving fifty clients in three to four hours of group calls a week, plus a little time answering questions outside of the calls. I was able to serve ten times the number of clients without increasing my workload by ten times.

If compound interest is the eighth wonder of the world, then I believe a bit of solid time leverage through a group coaching program must be the ninth. You can load a group coaching program with value that does not directly involve your time, such as additional guest coaches, a community and live events, which hugely enhances the experience for the client.

In the next section of the book, you will learn how to create Leverage, the L in the L.E.A.P Method, so that you can stop swapping your life for cash. I will also show you how I went from charging £2,777 for my group coaching program to $18,000 and got myself out of Low Ticket Land.

1. Scarily Unpredictable Income

If you start each month not knowing how many clients you're going to sign that month, then you're probably experiencing this problem. You're also in this situation if the amount of cash coming into your business varies wildly from month to month and without reason.

The solution to this is twofold.

Firstly, you need predictable sales. An evergreen marketing system generates this for you. As my clients and I have proven countless times, a good evergreen marketing system will deliver one to three, sometimes more, clients to you every week.

When you review some simple data points in your business, you'll discover how many leads need to come into your world for you to sign one client. Once you know this, signing three or even five clients a month becomes simple maths.

Secondly, setting up your offers so that they give you a monthly recurring revenue will provide your business with consistent cash. Your clients can sign up to a monthly payment plan to be part of your program. Monthly payment options also help the client who prefers to budget on a monthly basis and doesn't have the upfront cash to invest.

We'll cover elements of how to sell *and* deliver your group coaching program on evergreen, so you can build a simple, sustainable business without the stress of launches and not knowing if you can pay your bills next month.

2. Tumbleweed Instead of Leads

The third problem of the troublesome trifecta is lead generation. I cannot tell you how many coaches come to me wanting to go evergreen with a group coaching program, but they don't have a proper lead generation strategy in place. Their client attraction strategy relies on referrals, which is a wonderful compliment to their work but is difficult to rely on as their main source of clients.

The solution is to have sustainable and diversified sources of leads. One of my favourite ways to do this is to use a three-pronged approach that involves organic, partnership and paid traffic. When you have more than one source of clients, you are at much lower risk of your sales grinding to an abrupt halt when your social media account is hacked or your Facebook

Ad account is shut down. We'll cover the audience growth options in more depth in later chapters.

A Business Without a Pathway to Profit Is a Hobby and Not a Business

At the centre of the L.E.A.P. Method solution is Profit. When you have the other three pieces in place, the result is of course a healthy, profitable business.

The only caveat to your experience of implementing the L.E.A.P. method being positive is whether you self-sabotage your income as a result of your relationship with money and sense of inner safety with being able to receive and manage more than enough money. We'll cover this topic in more depth also, because it's such a core part of you experiencing the success you deserve.

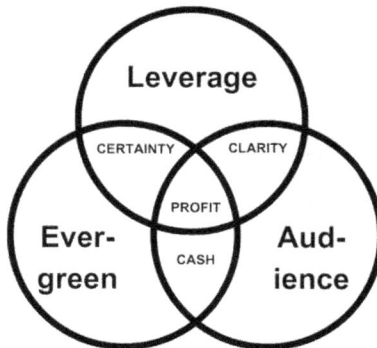

PART 2

LEVERAGE

3

HOW GROUP COACHING CAN AMPLIFY CLIENT RESULTS

Will a group coaching program work for your particular niche, and will clients get great results like they do from your one-to-one coaching right now?

MOST COACHES BELIEVE their clients get better results working with them one-to-one than in a group coaching program. I can see why you might think that if, right now, you're also sitting on that side of the fence.

As a coach, you naturally believe that you are the one who helps clients get results. However, instead of relying on one-to-one calls to create transformations with clients, it is entirely possible to create a group coaching environment that delivers the same – and even better – results than working with clients one at a time.

How is this possible, exactly?

Firstly, by leveraging the power of the community. When clients work with you one-to-one their learning is limited to just you, but in a community your clients have the opportunity to learn from others you've selected to join the group too. As long as you keep your ego in check about your clients learning from each other rather than just from you, this creates a rapid learning and transformation opportunity for your clients.

Think about it: if each of us is the average of the five people we spend the most time with, your clients' perspective of what's possible for them will explode when they join a high-level community.

Secondly, if you structure the curriculum and group calls effectively, you can provide a container for the biggest transformations.

When you craft your curriculum with a clear pathway for creating client results and learn how to run great group calls where everyone feels seen and supported, your group container can become even more valuable than a one-to-one experience with you. You can provide one-to-one support in a group coaching program, it just might not be private.

If you continue to believe that all your clients get the best results by working one-to-one with you and don't set up a group coaching offer, you limit your ability to grow your income and impact. Or worse, you launch a group offer and end up serving your clients in that coaching program as if they're one-to-one clients, and that's exhausting!

But when you design a group coaching container with better-than-one-to-one-results in mind, your program is able to become the go-to in your niche and you're able to create more income and impact while working less.

Is this still true even if your work with clients requires vulnerability?

Like one of my clients Lizzy, an Emotional and Binge Eating Coach and Founder of Luv Health, you might work with clients to help them solve really sensitive problems, which makes you doubt whether it's truly possible to help clients in a group environment.

If you've only ever worked with clients on a one-to-one basis like Lizzy had when she first started working with me, you might be putting the success of your program down to having ample one-to-one support and hand-holding from you.

Lizzy knew she was brilliant at helping her clients unpick and rewrite their personal limiting stories around food in a private conversation with her, and the opportunity to go deep in this way wasn't going to be so easy in a group setting. What Lizzy discovered through serving clients in a group program was that teaching her clients how to unpick and reframe their own stories by themselves, with lighter support from Lizzy, was a thousand times more empowering for her clients. It gave them a personal skill set they could take into their lives long after they finished the program with her, rather than being dependent on Lizzy to do this for them.

When you work on vulnerable topics with a client, it can be easy for that client to avoid doing the work because their barriers of internal resistance are too strong. This was Lizzy's fear when it came to moving from one-to-one to serving a group of clients. She didn't want to jeopardise her clients' transformations that she'd become known and trusted for. However, Lizzy discovered that the group format led her clients to become more self-sufficient, to find answers for themselves and occasionally to coach each other. These differences sped up and strengthened each client's transformation.

The other major hesitation you might have with group coaching if you work with sensitive topics is that your clients won't initially know each other, yet will be asked to feel comfortable enough to be vulnerable in front of others. Without the comfort, confidence and safety to be vulnerable and share things that may make them feel shameful, the depth of transformation for a client can fall short.

But Lizzy discovered that when one person shows vulnerability, it gives permission to other, newer clients to share what makes them feel vulnerable too. There's nothing like being fully and lovingly accepted by a community of people when you share something that feels shameful, emotional or makes you feel vulnerable. It is really powerful to know that you're not alone and there are real people out there who have experienced the same thing.

Since launching her group program, Lizzy has helped nearly seventy clients in the first twelve months, more than tripling the number of people she would have helped if she'd stayed serving her clients in a one-to-one container.

She discovered that her clients still get incredible results in a group format and no amount of one-to-one time would make up for any client's unwillingness to do the work, follow the process and take every step required to create a transformation in their relationship with food.

Lizzy says, "What surprised me about the group format is how much each client gets out of listening to the other clients' questions, challenges and experiences. A client's story can resonate with other clients. Even if they're way further ahead, it can remind them of where they've been and even remind them of things that they may still want to work on. The group also gives them all an opportunity to consistently hear similar messages, and to really get that into their system and their mindset."

Feeling safe in a group of other women can feel really difficult for some people, and can put them off becoming part of a transformational community of women altogether.

I've had more than my share of bullies, all of whom were women. Each situation, from preschool to even university level, made me feel insecure and excluded from the group. Like many women who experienced bullying at school, I became socially anxious around groups of women and didn't trust them.

Like a lot of women who struggled with bullying, the long-term results were damaging. I developed a subconscious belief that I wasn't safe around other women. Yet here I was building a business where I worked exclusively with women clients.

I worried I wasn't good enough and wondered what they were saying about me behind my back. It took me over a year through some trauma work to confront the alarming truth that I didn't feel safe with my own clients.

Talk about a complex juxtaposition happening inside me, contrasting my love for helping other women with my deep, untrusting fear of them.

Through trauma release work, I dismantled those deeply entrenched false beliefs. My personal experience is why I'm so intentional about the environment we cultivate inside my coaching programs. I hand-select everybody who enters the community to make sure they're fully aligned with our values and vibes. This means the women inside feel safe and invited to show up in all their messy, real, and vulnerable glory.

That, my friend, is the kind of community that's critical to those sexy, record-smashing breakthroughs that your coaching business deserves. It is also critical to your clients' results. Setting standards for how you desire your clients to show up for themselves and others inside the community will have a profound impact on their experience.

4

THE JOY AND ECONOMICS OF HIGH-TICKET GROUP COACHING

YOU MIGHT WORRY about what people think about your business. Do you have enough Instagram followers to look credible? Does your brand look professional but also approachable? Is your content going to annoy someone or cause you to get trolled by someone who is triggered by you?

Will your ideal client be able to afford high-ticket coaching? What if your family or friends find out what you're charging for your coaching and think you've got too big for your boots?

What would happen if you just continued to show up and do the damn thing despite those worries? You might find out it's nowhere near as bad as you think.

Like most brides, I felt nervous in the weeks leading up to our wedding. But maybe unlike most brides, I wasn't worried about the logistics of the day or potential drama with family. I was worried I wouldn't feel or look the way I wanted.

I initially judged myself for being concerned about something that seemed so vacuous and shallow. But after more than ten years of being horrendously body-conscious and struggling with various forms of disordered eating off the back of that, I realised my internal conflict made sense.

To make matters worse, I had five stunning bridesmaids who were all at least one size smaller than me. I had done so much inner work that led me to genuinely accept and love myself, including what I looked like, but there's nothing quite like a wedding – one where all eyes are on you – to bring back some of those old patterns.

Ironically, we totally blew my budget on gorgeous bridesmaid dresses because I wanted my friends to feel beautiful. And they really did look so beautiful! Nevertheless, it was a challenge to navigate those old patterns that bubbled up during the weeks before my wedding.

But guess what happened on the actual day? I showed up and finally got hitched, for starters. To my surprise, I felt good about myself. It might be a bit clichéd to say this about my wedding, but I had the time of my life. All my gut-wrenching worries about not looking or feeling great on my wedding day just didn't come to fruition.

That's the thing about worry – you can ruminate over so many things that either don't come to pass or turn out to be nowhere near as bad as you expect. In fact, like me, you might discover that you end up having the time of your life!

To put it in another context, I see this pattern again and again with clients who have been nervous about charging a high-ticket fee for their coaching. Initially, they're worried they'll price too many people out of working with them or it brings up huge feelings of imposter syndrome.

This was just like Caroline Stevens, Business Mentor to Cake Makers and Women Entrepreneurs. When Caroline came to work with me, she had a low-ticket membership for cake makers that sold for just £34 a month, so moving to selling a high-ticket group coaching program brought up all the typical fears about her audience's ability to afford something more expensive.

In her own words, Caroline said, "I told myself that cake makers can't afford to spend that amount of money, and I worried I'd launch it and get zero sales." But her fears didn't come true and she went on to sign six new clients into her group coaching program and made a total of £22,400 in the first month.

Her biggest surprise was just... "how easy it is to deliver on an ongoing basis. My curriculum is pre-recorded now. I previously thought it was more beneficial to deliver trainings live, but I've completely changed my mind on that. It's more valuable to have a potent ten-minute training that gets straight to the point than a one-hour live training. Doing it that way means our group calls each week are more powerful because we work through their questions together rather than having to focus on the training aspect. I realise it's a better way to help them. Now that my curriculum is created it literally takes me around three hours a week to maintain the program between the one-hour group call and answering questions in the Facebook group."

Despite her initial fears, Caroline loves serving highly committed clients in her group program, and she's able to go deeper with clients while making more money per hour. Her initial fears were misguided and running her high-ticket group program where new clients enrol every month on evergreen has been one of the most game-changing decisions in her business.

Is offering a high-ticket group coaching program right for you?

Most coaches get stuck selling low-ticket group coaching programs because they haven't learned how to sell high ticket – yet. Many entrepreneurs tell themselves they're "not ready to charge high ticket fees". You might be thinking that right now.

There are people out there less qualified than you who make more money and help more people, only because they simply decided to believe in themselves and go for it.

You have value and expertise that deserve to be paid good money for. It's simply a case of you recognising and packaging your expertise into the high-ticket offer that's appropriate for your niche and choosing to shift your beliefs and mindset into becoming the leader that's playing at that level of value.

And this is exactly how the CEO Coach thinks. Her mentality is this: "I want to step up and be paid well for the value that I deliver."

So what goes into a high-ticket group coaching program?

Most coaches assume that selling something high ticket means you've got to give clients lots of one-to-one time. This comes from the belief that because clients are paying more, you have to give them everything possible. However, this isn't what high-ticket clients are really paying for. I also see coaches giving their clients everything they've ever created – all the courses, all the bonuses, and their newborn puppy too, because they're trying to pack the offer with tonnes of value so they can feel as though it's actually worth the high-ticket price point.

This over-delivery is fuelled by imposter syndrome and self-doubt, rather than having the client's desires in mind. This isn't what high-ticket clients are buying. Frankly, your client just finds it overwhelming.

Another approach is to turn yourself into a L'Oreal advert and charge high ticket because the belief is that you're worth it. I'm not even going to give the time of day to that approach and reasoning for raising prices. Your worth is infinite, and yet the price of your coaching program should be based on the value to the client, not on your value as a totally unique one in eight billion humans on this planet.

The last thing I see happening is people making an offer high ticket just to make it exclusive, which only really works if you're a private members' club.

What's actually happening in all of these situations is that these coaches are struggling to articulate the value of their offer, so they struggle to command high-ticket investments.

This used to be me. I ran my accelerator program as if it was a one-to-one experience in a group format with three calls a week for just eight clients, direct messaging support and not enough personal boundaries from me, because I really, really care about people getting great results.

I believed that results came from my one-to-one time, but that's not true. I believed that my time was the income-generating asset, but in reality a coach's income-generating assets are their programs and process for getting client results.

This is the key here. It's your process. It's your intellectual property. Being able to package that up into your curriculum so clients can follow it, along with your personalised guidance, is really, really important.

To sum up, I learned that I did not need to do loads of one-to-one time to create great client results. In fact, *clients* create the best results within a group format, because they're inspired and supported by others along the way. In a group, you stop limiting your clients to learning just from you.

When designed effectively, group containers are deeply powerful. Most group containers are not designed well, though, so if you've been part of one before and were disappointed by the experience, don't let that put you off for life. That would be like going on a bad date and deciding never to date again.

High-ticket group coaching programs contain three core elements:

Your Curriculum

This is your secret sauce; it is your unique process for creating results with your clients and this is also your intellectual property. This is likely to include a clear success path that you've intentionally designed in a way to guide clients to their desired result in the fastest way possible.

This often looks like laying out clear phases or milestones for clients to follow at their own pace.

Live Q&A Coaching Calls

These calls are where the rubber meets the road. Whether they're weekly or biweekly calls, these sessions allow you to help clients implement the process, and allow you to really get to know each individual client.

The Curated Community

Beware of being a coach who lets any old person into their programs just because you want to make a sale. Your clients are investing in a high-ticket, high-value experience, so make sure it feels like that for them based on how you pre-qualify your clients. This gives your offer a built-in mastermind component which is a game-changer for most clients, and often a reason why they might renew and stay with you.

What's the difference between low- and high-ticket offers?

A low-ticket offer has an unclear or generic program promise, whereas a high-ticket offer has a very clear, valuable promise.

Your program promise is a single sentence statement that describes the result your client will get from your program when they go all in, implement what you teach and show up for themselves. The more specific you are with your program promise, the more valuable it will appear to your ideal client because they will know it's relevant to them.

Many coaches tie themselves in knots when it comes to identifying the specific outcome they help clients create. Often, that's because their clients have created all sorts of different outcomes in the past, so there's no real common theme. Or it's because the modalities they're trained in can be used for any number of problems.

However, the more determined you are to keep the outcome of your program vague, the more you'll stop yourself from making the money and impact you want to make with your clients. The value of the program simply isn't clear when the promise is vague. So place a stake in the ground and finally take a stand for what you can help your clients achieve.

For example, I could say that my Freedom Accelerator® program helps women entrepreneurs to grow their coaching business online, but that would be too vague for my ideal client to understand the value. Instead, the program promise is that it helps coaches to craft and scale a high-ticket group coaching program on evergreen so they can sign one, two, three or more new clients a week without needing to launch.

What if your work isn't as "tangible" as the business niches might be? If that's the case, you can still talk about specific, tangible outcomes in your programs, but the specificity may need to come from other parts of your messaging, such as the specific problem you help your client solve, for example: "I help women create freedom from binge and emotional eating."

Or you might talk about the specific person your ideal client is and the situation they are in, for example: "I help parents with strong-willed toddlers and a good cop/bad cop parenting dynamic to create sanity and peace in their home."

Perhaps you worry about making promises you might not be able to keep for your clients if they don't show up and do the actual work. You can solve this problem by making a tweak to make to your program promise.

Instead of saying, "I promise you will create *(insert specific, tangible result)* inside my program," say, "I promise I will teach you how to create *(insert specific, tangible result)* inside my program," because that is definitely a promise you can keep. Your client must always meet you halfway and implement what you teach them.

Another difference between low- and high-ticket offers is that low-ticket offers have a "catch-all" ideal client. For example, "any female entrepreneur" is not a strong enough ideal client to create a high-ticket offer for. I also find most ideal client avatar exercises don't work for high-ticket offers because they don't take into account the nuances that lead specific types of clients to invest at that level.

Low-ticket offers are similar to other programs and become a commodity in the market: the program is similar to many others. On the other hand, a high-ticket offer is unique in the market. There are many ways in which you can craft your offer in a unique way, including a unique approach for creating client results, offering in-person experiences, adding additional support and being incredibly specific with your program promise.

High-ticket offers focus on implementation over information. This is a really important differentiating factor because so much information is readily available for free online, such as on YouTube or podcasts, or it's available very cheaply through books. The real value in information is your client's ability to apply it to their lives to create a result. When your program focuses on implementation, you can charge a lot more for it.

A low-ticket offer is often a band-aid or a plaster (depending on whether you're American or British) because it doesn't give them a complete and comprehensive solution like a high-ticket offer does. A low-ticket offer leaves the client needing to invest in further support and other programs to reach the result they want. A high-ticket program gives a client more of what they need, without throwing the kitchen sink in.

Finally, a low-ticket offer is transactional in nature, whereas a high-ticket offer is transformational in nature. This means there is a real shift within the client, often in their identity, by the end of the process of working with you. They are genuinely transformed.

Chances are, you might be selling a weird hybrid between a low- and high-ticket offer right now. You meet some of these requirements but you're not meeting others, so you're still not able to charge a high-ticket fee comfortably and consistently. Or maybe you're selling a coaching offer that's got a low-ticket price point but you're delivering high-ticket value.

You don't get paid for the value you deliver, you get paid for the value you articulate, so you have to get good at articulating the value of your offer. A high-ticket offer has a clear, valuable promise, but most coaches struggle with this piece.

Here's an analogy for you: How much would you pay for a plane ticket in *any* potential seat to *anywhere* in the world? You could be flying from London to Edinburgh in economy or you could be going from London to Sydney in first class. How much would you pay for this Surprise Seat when you don't know what you are getting?

Compare this amount to how much you'd be willing to pay for a plane ticket from London to Sydney in first class. I bet you'd be willing to pay a lot more. That's the difference between a vague promise in your high-ticket offer versus a clear, valuable promise that your client is willing to pay a lot more for.

Do you need to sell low-ticket offers before selling high-ticket?

I always recommend learning how to attract your high-value clients first. Take the time to work out what messaging speaks most powerfully to them, what makes high-ticket clients buy and what offer they are excited to invest in. Then create a down-sell offer later to serve anyone who isn't ready to work with you in a high-ticket container yet.

You can sell high-ticket offers first. I did. You do not need to sell low ticket to earn the right to sell high ticket. In fact, I believe you're better off learning how to sell high ticket. That way, you can grow your audience with high-ticket clients from the get-go, because you're speaking their language in your messaging. Otherwise, you're like Walmart trying to become Wholefoods.

It isn't easier to sell low ticket than high ticket. People don't buy because it's cheap, they buy because they see value.

There will always be low-ticket clients in your audience. There is no rush to serve them right now even though you may feel surrounded by them. They will still be there in six or twelve months' time. In fact, there will probably be many more of them in that time as your audience grows. So in the meantime, focus on mastering the art of crafting and selling high-ticket offers first. This will generate more cash into your business and fuel more growth for you in a much shorter time.

What if your audience can't afford high-ticket investments?

There are clients at every price point. When you position your offer well, it attracts the right people. When you believe your audience can't afford it, what you're doing is listening to the people in your audience that tell you they don't have the money right now.

You will naturally hear that from some people, because generally speaking, saying that you don't have the money to purchase something is a normal and socially accepted sales objection. What you won't ever hear from your audience is, "Hey Rose, offer something ten times the price so I can buy it, please."

There are people in your audience right now waiting for you to offer a transformational program at a higher price point. But you're listening to the other people saying they don't have the money. And the people that do have the money are simply silent.

While you continue to argue for your clients' limitations by telling yourself the people in your audience don't have the money, other entrepreneurs offering similar programs to yours are taking a stand for your potential clients' possibilities and are learning how to sell high-ticket offers to them. As a result, you miss out on serving your most committed clients in a high-ticket container.

You have created your current social media audience through the messaging you've been sharing online and through the prices you've been selling at. You can shift and grow your audience towards a group of people who can afford and want to invest at a high-ticket level and are excited to pay high-ticket fees for what you offer. You have that choice and you have that power. Don't limit your business or your pricing based on the audience that you have right now, because your audience can change.

So just like I approached my wedding day with fearful trepidation, if you feel the same about raising your rates and charging high-ticket fees for your group coaching program, keep taking steps forward anyway. Chances are, it won't be anywhere near as scary as you think… and you might even realise you love it more than any offer you've sold before.

5

FROM CHARGING £2,777 TO $18,000

IF YOU'VE EVER FOUND yourself tied in knots about your pricing strategy, I get it. I must receive a question about pricing at least a couple of times a week. Before we talk about how to determine your pricing, let's cover the four pricing mistakes you must avoid.

Firstly, deciding your price based on other people's pricing strategies is not a recipe for success. Whether you're researching the market to match your price to similar programs, or making yourself the cheapest in the market in an attempt to undercut the competition, neither approach does you justice. When you decide your price based on other people's limited view of money, themselves and their clients, you create more limitations for yourself.

Secondly and similarly, don't crowdsource your pricing by asking potential clients what they would be willing to pay. When you ask someone what they'd be willing to invest, most people can't help but think about what money they have in their bank account right now and how much of that they'd be willing to spend. Therefore, they give you a lowball number. You'll always end up with a mediocre result that doesn't reflect the true value they place on transforming a situation they care about.

Their lowball response has nothing to do with how resourceful they are when they want to invest in something that matters to them. Your clients will be far more resourceful than simply using the current cash in their bank when they come to purchase from you. I've seen people do some seriously impressive things to make it possible to invest in themselves and work with me.

Thirdly, don't make your group program longer so it feels reasonable to charge more for it. People will in fact pay more for faster results. So if you can create a result with a client within a month or two, and you don't need to do three months or six months with them, then you can charge a chunk of money for those one or two months. People pay for speed.

Fourthly, you don't necessarily have to make your group coaching program cheaper than your one-to-one. Coaches sometimes get fully booked in their one-to-one and then launch a group coaching program at half the price because they've had a number of people say they can't afford their one-to-one.

They assume that selling their group coaching program at a lower fee would serve these people. But what ends up happening is that this coach signs the same number of people who say they would normally sign into their one-to-one. The coach only makes half the money and that doesn't feel so good. The people who say they can't afford to work with you right now will do one of three things. They will either wait until they can, buy a much lower ticket course from you or find an alternative option. There are more than enough clients for you to charge the prices you want to charge.

In this situation, my recommendation is to double or even triple your one-to-one price when you launch your group offer, and then sell your new group coaching program at your old one-to-one price.

At this point you're probably pretty comfortable with selling an offer at your current one-to-one rate. You can stack a lot more value into a group coaching program versus a one-to-one program with you, which warrants a high fee anyway. And just because someone cannot afford to work with you right now, that doesn't mean they never will.

The Journey From £2,777 to $18,000

I first sold my flagship program, the Freedom Accelerator, for £2,777 (around USD $3,000) back in March 2020. To be honest, I was terrified.

I was terrified of clients not getting results and feeling like I'd failed them. I was terrified of what it would feel like to talk to more than one person at once on a Zoom call. I was terrified of handling the workload of a group program as well as a fully booked private coaching roster. Yet today, I regularly sell a place on that same program for $18,000 without any concern.

There's a lot to be said about how your confidence increases over time when it comes to your pricing and successfully delivering a group container. No matter how scared you might feel about selling and delivering a group coaching program right now because it's so new to you, I promise you will climb the top of that Ladder of Believability if you just keep taking one step at a time.

Each step up that belief ladder is another step away from fear and self-doubt, and a step closer to confidence and certainty in your offer, your ability to serve clients and your price point. As you climb that ladder, you'll find that you attain new levels of belief about your pricing and have the urge to charge more to match that new level of certainty because you know you can deliver great results with your clients.

Equally, you can find yourself falling back down the ladder if you receive negative feedback from a client, a refund request or if you feel your clients aren't getting the results you want them to have. Just because these things might happen (and they most likely will at some point), it does not mean that you will inevitably lose confidence in your group and pricing. It is entirely up to you whether these negative events happen.

You either take that client feedback or situation and turn it into all the reasons why you and your program suck, to the point that you want to throw the business in the trash and go and live in a hammock in Bali forever more... or you turn that worst-case scenario into the best thing that ever happened to you in your business.

A refund request once triggered me into weeks of self-doubt, low confidence and an inability to confidently sell my program. I turned this into a $200,000 sales month the following month, despite my previous biggest sales month being less than a third of that.

When you end up in the depths of your self-doubt, questioning whether you're really cut out to be a great coach, to run a wildly successful business and deal with all the different personalities that come with that, you have one of two choices. Either you stay in the pits of that spiral of negative thinking and talk yourself out of your dreams of leading the business you desire, or you climb back out of the hole and get yourself into an upward spiral of thinking that leads to stronger belief and confidence in yourself than ever before.

Having gone up and down in those spirals myself, I know that you cannot feel and truly anchor in the highest of highs without first going to the deepest of depths in your own mind about your abilities to run a business, help clients and do it all with integrity. When you go to that deep level of self-questioning, you either stay there and crash out of your business, or you see it as an invitation to bounce back with stronger resolve than ever before to achieve your big dream. I call this ability to bounce back stronger than ever before *relentlessness*. You may call it something else.

It is critical to have fantastic coaching support and personalised guidance in these situations.

Running a seven-figure business is seen as flashy, sexy and exciting. And it can be all of that. But it also requires you to handle multiple difficult situations with poise, presence and a CEO's most important tool in their toolkit: processes. If you're not being mentored by someone who has learned to handle all kinds of situations effectively, ethically, and in alignment with their values, who can also guide you on how to regulate your nervous system, find a mentor who can. It will save you a lot of money but, most importantly, it will save you a lot of emotional heartache and, quite possibly, your livelihood too.

Don't let one or two misaligned clients take your dream away from you. Take the feedback on board but check in with yourself first before taking on board *all* feedback as if it is the absolute truth. And never, ever do or do not do something in your business because of what someone else might think or say about it. This is the golden rule.

As you move up the Ladder of Believability, you'll find yourself wanting to increase the price you're charging, but there's more to a price increase than simply having the feeling that you want to increase it. Here's what I learned about price increases on my journey to charging $18,000.

1. The less vague your program promise is, the more you can charge.

The clearer your program promise, the more you can charge. When it first launched, the Freedom Accelerator was a fairly generic business coaching program. I wasn't that clear on what I was promising to people other than "let me teach you how to sign more clients and grow your business".

As soon as I narrowed the program promise down to teaching clients how to start and scale group coaching programs on evergreen, the perceived value of the program skyrocketed and so could the investment.

2. Raise your price when you increase the amount of real value to your clients.

When I made the shift in the program's promise, I doubled the length of the program because the outcome I was promising was a big one. I wanted to give enough space and time to helping clients achieve that promised result. I also doubled the investment when I doubled the length of the program but the price increase was less about the length of the program and more about the value of the result I was promising.

Worst case scenario, if a client launched and evergreened their program in two to three months (which many have since done), they then had nine to ten more months of support from me to truly scale that result to the moon. Rather than just help them sell their program, I wanted to help them with the client delivery aspects of it, scale it, and challenge them to go even further inside their business. I knew my clients were going to face challenges along the way and I wanted to be able to support them through those challenges.

Having this huge amount of additional value to them in mind, doubling the investment from £5-6,000 for six months to £10-12,000 for a whole year made sense.

Please note that I didn't load up the program with extra trainings, bonuses and other random things to try to increase the value. This doesn't actually add value to your clients; it simply gives them more to do.

3. You do not need to stop your current program to relaunch it with an updated promise and new pricing.

When the program promise was narrowed down, I rebuilt the curriculum (for the third time) so I could deliver on that promise. I didn't close the program and re-open it a few months later. I kept consistently signing clients into it and rebuilt the plane as I was flying it.

Current clients get access to the newer version which often delights them because they're able to travel even further in their journey through these upgrades. For you, it means you can avoid a lull in sales because you don't have the stop/start kangaroo juice like a car that's not in gear properly. Therein lies the third lesson: you do not need to stop and start or relaunch a program every time you want to make a change to it.

As a practical example, let's say you currently have ten clients in your program, each with a different period of time left with you as they all joined at different times over the last few months. You've realised you want to narrow down on your program promise and upgrade your curriculum to reflect this. The update isn't a huge departure from what you currently deliver and it's almost certainly an upgrade for your clients in terms of what they will experience and learn from you. In these conditions, sharing the upgrades with your clients means everyone wins as they get access to the newer version of the program without paying the higher price, and you're able to continue to make sales because you don't close it.

Unless your program promise is massively changing, you don't need to close the current program and you can simply refine the one that's already in motion. This may fly in the face of what you have been taught but it's clear that everyone gets to win by taking this approach.

4. When you grow personally, your prices can too.

When you've invested a lot in your own learning and growth, you're able to take clients really far in their own journey.

I've invested over $300,000 (~£250,000) into my own learning and mentorship up to this point and over the five years I've spent committing to mastery in my own work, I've learned a lot. So by the time I was at the stage of raising my prices again from £10-12,000 to $15-18,000 (~£12-15,000), I knew I had a deep well of life-changing value to give others. It also confirmed the increase in the length of the program because for me to share that value with clients, we would need at least a twelve-month container together.

If you're a true expert at what you do, have many years of experience, have invested a lot in your own learning or have helped a large number of clients to create results, your prices probably need to go up too.

Equally, communicating to your audience *why* you're an expert puts your pricing into context. Your potential clients won't know if you're an expert or not unless you give them reasons to believe you are. Don't be afraid to share your personal stories that show you're an expert. People do care about those stories, so don't brush them away and assume nobody cares or that your ideal client would consider it boasting.

I ignored the time I spent at McKinsey & Co. and believed my future clients wouldn't care about that piece of my story. In reality, my ideal client often loves knowing I have that background, and the same will be true about your unique background and story of expertise too. Your ideal client does give a monkey's!

5. Choose the currency that works best for you, and that might not be USD.

I shifted from GBP to USD for a couple of reasons. When we moved from the UK to Lisbon, we began living our lives in Euros, and still paying team costs in both GBP and USD. At this point, any of the three currencies would have worked as our pricing currency.

I have clients in the UK, the USA, Canada and in countries across Europe, Asia and Australia as well. Given we're a global company and have clients all across the world, I chose the US dollar as my pricing currency because every one of my clients is familiar with the US dollar.

The Brits and the Europeans know they can apply that mental discount in their heads from USD to GBP or EUR, which feels good. The Canadians are very used to working with the USD and of course, it made no difference to those from the United States.

However, if most of your business costs are in your local currency, I would recommend pricing in your local currency for your high-ticket offers because the foreign exchange fees and exchange volatility mean you risk losing out.

6. You may need to upgrade your ideal client when you raise your rates.

I know it to be true that your messaging will predominantly call in a certain type of client. If that type of client more often than not genuinely cannot afford to work with you, or more importantly, the value of their perceived upside from working with you does not warrant the fee you're asking, then it's time to upgrade your ideal client and messaging. For me, when I raised my prices this meant I needed to speak to those who were further on in their business journey in my messaging.

In this sense, pricing is a market positioning tool. By choosing your price point, you choose to play within a certain position in the market. In other words, do you want to be a Walmart or a Wholefoods? An Asda or a Harrods Food Hall?

7. If you begrudge the value you give for the amount you're being paid, raise your rates immediately.

I soon felt underpaid at £10,000-12,000 and nudged the investment up to $15,000-$18,000 (~£12-15,000) to reflect the level of value available to those who took the leap for themselves and decided to walk with me on their own path to success.

When you take transaction fees of three to five percent into account, taxes, the operational costs of delivery, as well as your marketing costs, you may realise you're not being paid fairly for what you're delivering. If that's the case, you can easily block your own sales even if you really want to sign new clients. If the price you're charging is too low, a part of you won't want to make that sale and you'll end up sabotaging it in some way.

I've seen this pattern a lot in my own clients. Paradoxically, the solution is to raise their rates, even when they're not signing the number of clients they want. Once you're in alignment with your price point, the floodgates get to open. Until then, feeling underpaid is not a recipe for receiving more clients at the same price point.

8. The more unique your program is, the more you can charge for it.

If your coaching program is like many other programs in the market with a similar program promise and ideal client, you're simply selling a commodity. It's like selling wheat or cotton on the stock exchange. It would be difficult to price your batch of wheat above the going market rate for wheat unless your wheat was different and special in some way.

The same applies to group coaching programs. If your program promise is different from other programs out there and the result you're helping people create is unique, there is more potential for you to charge more.

There's nothing wrong with having a commodity program in your business; I have one called the Clarity and Clients Bootcamp. It's similar to a lot of other programs out there, in that its program promise is to help newer coaches sign their first or next three to five high-value clients without using paid traffic.

There is definitely a ceiling on the price point for that program. I probably couldn't consistently sell it for $10,000.

9. The higher the value of the result you help clients achieve, the more you can charge for it.

You might hate me a little for this because value is so subjective. This can make calculating the program's value to your client incredibly difficult.

Think about your ideal client and the result you create with them in the program: the impact that has on their life, their happiness, their relationships, their health, and their future – what is the value of that to them? Can you estimate a monetary value for it?

Chances are, if your client went through your program and followed it to the best of their ability, the value of their result would be massive. That means, when you increase the value of what you do with clients, you can increase your price point in line with that, too.

That does not mean you should stack your program full of additional components, such as extra one-to-one calls, all the courses you ever created or other random things, just so you can increase the price point for it. Instead, look at defining it as the value of the result you help somebody create. That's the thing they will be really aware of when they make that investment. They will look at the price versus the result they will create with your support.

When you communicate the value of your program clearly to a potential client in a way that connects with them, and then share the price within that context, you'll eradicate all money objections and they'll ask you how they can sign up. Also, you'll feel great that you're delivering a service that goes far beyond the price your client has paid.

6

MY $140,000 MISSED OPPORTUNITY

LET me share with you exactly what launching did to my business. It wasn't pretty.

This chart shows the amount of cash I received per month for twelve months from April 2020 when I was still launching my group coaching programs. To be clear, I am not sharing from a place of "look at me, I made all this money". These numbers might represent a lot of money or very little to you. Either way, don't let the size of the numbers throw you off. Focus on the pattern.

Cash Received

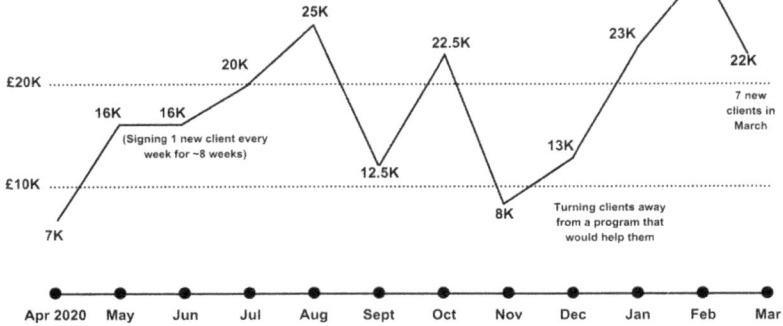

What is "cash received" and why does it matter?

Cash received is the total amount of money you received into your business bank account that month. This figure can very easily be different from your agreed sales value that month. For example, you might sign a $12,000 client but they only pay you $2,000 in the first month of their six-month payment plan. In this situation, your cash received is $2,000 and your sales value is $12,000.

When you have really inconsistent cash coming into your business, you struggle to make hiring decisions, because you're not sure you can commit to paying someone every month. This then stops you from scaling, because you can't do it all yourself. Even if you're not looking to hire more team members, inconsistent cash (and low cash in general) holds you back from reinvesting back into the business to generate more growth. Having really high cash months can also lure you into a false sense of security. You feel like your business is really successful in your launch months, which can lead you to increase your lifestyle costs now that you have more cash to splash, but when the dust settles you find you can't keep up the lifestyle upgrades unless you have another successful launch.

Ultimately, cash is the lifeblood of your business, and inconsistent cash causes huge financial stress, which is simply not fun.

When I put my cash received information on a chart, it blew my mind. I could clearly see where I was implementing an evergreen marketing model and where I was using launches to sell my group coaching program.

Let me walk you through this. April 2022 was right after the pandemic hit and it all went a bit tits up. We had £7,000 cash received in that month. Then I implemented an evergreen funnel for the first time and I signed one new client every single week for nine weeks in a row into my high-ticket group coaching program which was around $5,000 at the time.

This was an incredibly profitable funnel for me. I started hitting consistent $16,000 months plus a $20,000 month soon after, as the payment plans began to stack over time. I was spending just $30 a day on Facebook Ads and bringing in a new client worth thousands every week.

We moved into a launch for a new low-ticket group coaching program at the beginning of August. You can see the launch month happened in August because the cash received spiked at that point from all the new payments. It was a great launch and I created $36,000 in sales value in that month.

I hadn't got the evergreen marketing system properly turned back on by September, though, and because a lot of new clients had paid in full during the launch, I had a pretty terrible cash month right after the launch. I took advice and turned the evergreen funnel off while the launch was happening, which was the wrong move because it simply didn't go back on the way it came off.

Being newer to the online marketing game, I didn't know what to look at to get the evergreen system working again and I ended up flustered and confused about why it wasn't working the way I expected it to. The low cash month didn't help my confidence either and the feeling of success from the launch the month before was long gone. In a bit of panic, I went back into a launch again in October which created more cash again and that's what you see in the chart.

What happened next is *fascinating*.

I took the same challenge launch that I implemented back in August, and I ran exactly the same process in October for the same program. I used the same forty launch emails, the same challenge content, the same webinar, the same scripts, the same everything, plus a couple of minor upgrade tweaks. Then we added in extra income-creating opportunities, such as a bump offer and a down sell on the checkout, so I added in more opportunities to make money from a proven, profitable launch that I'd done previously. It was great fun. I loved it.

I do not advocate for evergreen marketing from a place of hating launches and having being burned by them. I teach from a place of having loved launching, and having loved selling on evergreen, but evergreen wins hands down every time. This cash chart is one of the reasons why that is the case.

We implemented exactly the same launch method in October and I was expecting similar results, if not better. I doubled my Facebook ad spend, expecting double the sales results given we would be increasing the number of people coming into the launch. Guess how much the sales value from that launch was. Just $11,000!

It was only a *third* of what we'd done a few months previously. I grew my audience in between and had done all the things you're meant to do between launches to support the chances of your next launch doing well. The only reason it says $22,000 in cash received on the chart for October is because I salvaged the situation by signing some one-to-one clients that month.

I had implemented exactly the same launch strategy, the same scripts... everything was exactly the same but I created entirely different results. I learned a valuable lesson: launches are very unpredictable.

Just because a launch does well once, it is not necessarily going to do well for you continually. That means when you rely on launching as the main marketing strategy, you're in for one hell of a ride in your coaching business.

This is terrifying for most business owners who have regular bills to pay, and is not a great way to build a sustainable business.

November was an "Oh crap" situation for me again. December was not too bad, but it was frustrating because back in May, June and July we had been doing well financially.

When the cash dries up, as it did for us towards the end of 2020, it creates financial stress for people without a back-up cushion. I was left licking my wounds and trying to figure out what to do next.

Since sharing this story, I've learned that I am not alone in this experience. Many other launch-based coaches have experienced the same situation of declining launch results and issues with cash flow.

The crazy thing was that I was turning clients away during this low period who wanted to buy a program that would help them, just because when I'd launched the offer in October I had decided to run the program in a cohort style so it was closed to new clients. I was *turning clients away* who wanted to join me in that program and purchase there and then. I had to tell them that I'd be launching it again in two or three months' time and ask them to wait until February or March, which broke my heart because I knew I could help them.

I decided to turn the evergreen funnel back on in January to March, which you can see on the chart where the cash started stacking back up. But by that point, I had already missed out on over $140,000 worth of sales. If I'd simply stuck with my evergreen funnel back in July and allowed the results to compound, by the end of the year I would have been $140,000 better off. I had been so conditioned to believe that launching was the best way to grow a coaching business that I missed out on the ease, income and client impact that could have been.

So what happened in February? That month, I implemented something I now fondly call the Anti-Launch Method, which was the laziest but most profitable and hilariously fun non-launch launch I've ever done in my life. Doing this requires no sales page, no webinar, no forty-email sequence, and no frolicking around the internet like a magical pony. All it requires is a Direct Messaging script and a good call to action to your audience. I now love teaching this to my clients as a back-pocket strategy.

The evergreen funnel continued to compound. In March, we had seven new clients join me in my different group programs, an average of between one and two new clients every week. No launching. Just chill. Going evergreen allowed me to stack payment plans and scale my business without all the extra effort required in a launch. Being able to sign a gentle stream of clients every week also gives you consistent cash received to reinvest and safely pay yourself well from the business without jeopardising it.

How did I first discover this magical land of evergreen funnels?

You're probably familiar with what a lead magnet is. You offer a free resource, often in the form of an e-book, PDF cheat sheet or even a short audio, in return for someone's name and email address to add to your email list.

I had built a PDF-style lead magnet and popped it on an Ad that initially led to a simple funnel. However, it wasn't converting into sales calls and sales into the main group coaching program on the back end of the funnel, at least not as much as I wanted it to.

As I was falling asleep one night, a random idea popped into my head. What if I invited people who signed up to my PDF lead magnet to watch a free training? I woke up the next morning, thankfully remembered the fleeting thought, and set about adding a second step into the funnel: a short webinar with a pitch to book a call with me.

And it *worked*.

Things have evolved a lot since early 2020 when it comes to evergreen webinar funnels and in my business we're constantly pioneering different approaches and strategies to stay ahead of the curve and feed that insight to my clients. What worked in 2020 doesn't work so well now, as the marketing landscape is always changing.

But I look back at that first evergreen funnel as a massive breakthrough. I was hooked on the power of creating a simple marketing system that would deliver applications and qualified sales calls into my calendar while I was sleeping.

As I write this for you now, over the last year we have typically spent $2,000-4,000 on Ads every month and have created $60,000-97,000 back in cash received per month. That's twenty to thirty times return on Ad spend. This is utterly bonkers given that the industry standard for Return On Ad Spend (ROAS) is typically five to ten times your Ad spend. In other words, most coaches who use Ads expect to have to pay $1-2 to get $5-10 back in revenue.

These results aren't because I have a massive online community of buyers. In fact, I started out with zero social media audience and had just my colleagues on LinkedIn and old friends on Facebook. At the time of writing, I don't have a big TikTok audience, a popular YouTube channel, or a huge email list. I have fewer than nine thousand followers on Instagram and I'll tell you this: they're not a very engaged bunch!

So if you're in the same position, don't fret. You can leverage Ads to build your audience, and it makes sense to do that when you can see that they're likely going to be profitable because your offer and messaging are clear.

I put our industry-leading results down to the power of a few things. Two of those things are:

1. We test simple tweaks in the funnel that make minor improvements which compound over time.

Each part of the funnel is a lever you can pull to increase your results and overall profitability. For example, when we changed something that felt really minor – the text on the application button – we doubled the number of people who clicked it. This had a huge impact overall by doubling the number of applications we received.

2. We keep repeating our messaging again and again.

My friends joke with me that I repeat myself all the time online, and it's partly true because I've been saying the same things again and again for the last two years like a creative broken record. Even if you feel like you've already said it all before, there are still people entering your online world today who need to hear it all again. There are still hundreds of thousands of people for you to share your message with.

Don't be afraid to repeat yourself many times, but keep the creative joy in your content creation process when you do, so it never feels stale or boring for you. When you add a strong organic content strategy to your paid traffic, your results will explode. When your online presence matches your Ads and your funnel, people will know they can trust you.

PART 3

EVERGREEN

7

SET YOURSELF UP FOR FREEDOM

A LOT of business coaches talk about helping you create more freedom in your business but don't live a freedom-based life-style themselves *and* still grow their business with happy clients.

A little while ago, I flew to South Africa for a long weekend on my husband's work trip. We went on safari and walked with and fed rescued elephants after breakfast in the stunning game reserve. In the meantime, a client was celebrating how, after having been in many different group coaching programs and masterminds before, she had never felt so supported by a mentor or group than inside my Freedom Accelerator.

Having this client share how she felt in this way flies in the face of the belief, and even fear, that you are not safe to enjoy your life and to take breaks without your clients feeling aban-doned, unsupported or even annoyed at you. I used to worry about this so much that I would find myself working far too much during my supposed "time off" from a place of fear.

Now I realise that the things you do outside of client delivery work actually deeply serve your clients too. It sets them an example of being able to take a break without working all the way through a holiday. Go after your own big goals in your business, such as leading a live event, launching a podcast or YouTube channel, publishing a book or landing speaking gigs. The time you spend on these activities isn't taking away from your clients: it contributes to your clients because it shows them what's possible too.

Equally, resting or taking a spa day in the middle of the week is part of delivering incredible support to your clients because if you're not well rested, you're not going to be able to show up for your clients in the best way possible. A frazzled, tired, overwhelmed coach is not what your clients want.

Freedom looks different for everyone.

You may not want to go on safari for the weekend. You may prefer to simply switch off from the business and spend time with your children or grandparents. You might be tempted by a yoga retreat or silent escape experience in the Costa Rican jungle. Or like some of my clients, you might also have a job as an actress or singer-songwriter and need to take dedicated time out to pursue those dreams.

I know it to be true that, when designed with client results and your personal lifestyle goals in mind, a group coaching program on evergreen is one of the simplest ways to create genuine freedom in your life. If you're prone to worrying about what your clients will think if you're not there for them twenty-four/seven, take a loving permission slip from me to look after yourself, pursue your big goals outside of client delivery and know that you're not only safe to do that, but that it also serves your clients too.

During the trip to South Africa, we received two strong applications to work with me through our evergreen funnel. These applications didn't come through because I was sharing my fancy trip on social media in a bid to generate demand for what I offer. I have nothing against doing that, but I enjoyed the fact that these leads were sold on the trustworthy solution I offer, rather than a snippet of a fancy lifestyle.

When I landed back in London, I received a message from someone I had spoken to the week before saying she was ready to get started on working together. I also had more requests for application calls with me than calendar space for the next two weeks. I'm not sharing this to show off. I'm sharing this to show you what's truly possible when you decide to build a business that runs on evergreen. Don't ever, ever give up on the dream life you desire.

You may be wondering how those two applications found their way into my inbox. The journey is pretty simple:

1. Potential new client is in pain and is open to hearing a solution.
2. They scroll through their social media and see an Ad that speaks directly to their pain or big desires and introduces the solution.
3. They click on this Ad to take the next step and find out more about the solution they've just been told about.
4. A landing page pops up and invites them to share their name and email address in exchange for a free

video training that will help them and teach them more about the solution to their problem.

5. The video delivers on that promise and then invites them again to take the next step in the form of an application to find out more details about the program that's designed for them.

There are various formats for an evergreen funnel, but this is one of my favourites because it's simple and therefore quick to get launched. An evergreen funnel just like this has generated multiple millions for me and my clients over the years in an incredibly profitable way.

What Evergreen Program Delivery Looks Like

Sometimes people assume that being evergreen with your program delivery simply means that your client has purchased a self-serve, passive course where there is no further involvement from you.

If you're selling a high-ticket group coaching program, this isn't the case. High-ticket evergreen is different from low-ticket evergreen and I'm a big advocate for the former because it supports much bigger results with your clients. I don't know about you, but I'm in the business of creating transformations, rather than just "selling stuff".

Here's an insight into what high-ticket evergreen client delivery can look like.

You first need an automated and streamlined onboarding process that can deal with ten or more new clients in one day.

You may never sign ten clients in a day, but that figure is a good stress test for your onboarding system. Automation to streamline onboarding is key because that gives you time and space to add in the personalisation that's going to make the client know they're valued. This means using easy and cheap software to send contracts automatically, to send onboarding emails in a timely manner, and to prompt an assistant to do the manual steps such as welcoming them into the community.

A critical piece of a successful evergreen program delivery is an onboarding section inside your curriculum that sets expectations with your clients, shares how to make the most of the program and explains the ways in which they're supported by you.

In terms of program delivery, you're looking at a maximum of five hours a week, and sometimes a lot less once you're in the swing of it. This depends on the size of your group, of course, but as the number grows you will probably want to bring on support coaches to expand your delivery capacity.

Your program delivery time might include a fortnightly or weekly group call, building or updating the curriculum, and answering questions in a community space outside of the calls. You may also have expert program coaches running additional calls for your clients, building curriculum or answering questions outside of calls. Find what you love doing the most when it comes to supporting clients and do that. Where do you add the most value to your clients with your unique set of skills?

You might be worried about needing to be on calls year-round, because you want to take holidays and breaks. And you absolutely can. I take vacations and have program coaches fill any gaps so my clients are always supported. I know of coaches who have brought their peers in to deliver their programs while on maternity leave for three months.

There are group coaching programs out there for $24,000 a year with only three group calls a month. You get to decide the rules. You get to decide what you believe will be best for your particular clients and it's totally workable with a bit of creative thinking.

The most important thing to get clear on is what will actually help your clients create results. You might assume right now that they need lots of time from you, but is that really the case? When you're clear on what your clients actually require to create transformations, you can reverse engineer that pathway for them without as much involvement from you, if that's what you desire.

I personally love being in the detail with clients and really getting to know each of them well so I can spot their self-sabotages, help them identify their unique opportunities and lovingly call them out on their BS. I know other coaches who prefer to stay in a more teaching-based role without getting into the nitty gritty of coaching, because that's where their brilliance lies. I also know coaches who have team members do all of their client delivery.

How do new clients slot in if the program is already in motion?

If you haven't been part of a group coaching program with open evergreen enrolment, you might wonder how it all works in practice for a new client who is joining a party that's already got started.

The fundamental switch that you must make for evergreen delivery to work is to stop teaching your curriculum on live training calls week-on-week. Move it into pre-recorded trainings that are instant-access for your clients. This has the benefit of changing long live trainings (perhaps sixty to ninety minutes) into five-to-twenty-minute nuggets of action-orientated videos. In a high-ticket container your clients are typically paying for implementation over sitting through hours of information.

You can also deliver these recorded training sessions with a wider variety of learning styles in mind, such as providing transcripts, workbooks, templates, differing speeds on the videos and purely audio-based options. This has the benefit of supporting people who learn in different ways.

When you move the curriculum into an instant-access version, you free up the call time for deep dive question and answer sessions in which you can meet your client where they're at in whatever stage of the process they may be. When a new client joins the calls, they learn from the questions of other people who are further ahead, while still getting solutions to their current challenges.

You might also worry about ruining the "group flow" if new clients are added in every month. But here's the thing: adding new people confirms your current clients' investment decisions and brings fresh energy to the group. Everyone has paid to have exclusive access to a curated community. Your clients trust you to bring in new people who fit the group in some way, who may bring a different perspective or have a different background, but still align with the rest of the community. Your clients know that the next client who joins could well be a new friend or collaborator in some way.

After hosting my first client retreat, a number of the women told me they were amazed at how different they were from each other but at the same time, how similar they all felt. This was because there was alignment and similarities in their values. When you share your values and what's most important to you in your marketing and sales process, you naturally attract similar people and repel those who don't quite align.

Do you need to launch your program a few times before turning it evergreen?

The short answer to this common question is: No.

I never did this and many of my clients don't either. You can evergreen your group program within a couple of weeks with a bit of thinking ahead. When I launched my high-ticket group offer the first time, I evergreened it straight away.

Knowing that you can make improvements to your program while you're delivering it means you don't need to beta run it a few times first. By all means, take that approach if you want to but it's not necessary. In most cases, when you beta run something, you end up closing the doors and reducing your ability to make new sales, which causes the cash rollercoaster problem all over again and can mean you turn clients away instead of serving them.

8

RECEIVE, RECEIVE, RECEIVE WITH FEMININE-LED SALES

I SAT in one of my favourite brunch locations in Lisbon on a hot summer afternoon, tapping away on my laptop and eating banana bread smothered in fresh honey. An unfamiliar voice next to me asked, "Are you a coach?"

I turned and saw a woman alone at the table next to me. I answered her and the conversation continued into a wonderful chat about her, her business and her past career. She'd built a successful coaching business helping others find freedom from chronic pain with a mind-body solution, just like she had done for herself.

She had her evergreen marketing system up and running but wasn't quite getting the results she wanted yet and was quizzing me on what I thought she should do next. I gave her my thoughts and she asked my name. To our amazement, we had the same name.

After connecting on Instagram, she left and I went on with my day, thinking nothing more of it. A few weeks later, an application landed in my email inbox from Rose and we hopped on Zoom together to chat through working together.

Our sales conversation ended up being a hugely powerful conversation through which I truly learned the difference between masculine and feminine sales for myself. I could see Rose wanted to jump in and work together but something was holding her back, so I asked her what it was. She replied, "I think I'm waiting for you to hard sell me."

And this was when the breakthrough came.

Rose had been coached to hard sell her prospects into working with her by a previous coach but her clients were in a vulnerable place when they came to her, so it wasn't working.

I responded by saying that I don't hard sell people and I told her that she had to lean in, rather than me pull or "bend her arm" in. For her to lean in and take the leap for herself, rather than for me to pull her off the ledge, required her to trust herself, rather than trust me over her own instincts.

She took the leap.

By modelling just a small part of what it means to lead with the feminine in sales conversations, clients like Rose are able to take that experience and add it into their own sales call. Rose was able to take that experience and add it into her own sales call.

Feminine-led sales attracts and pulls clients in, whereas masculine-led sales is more outbound-orientated with direct outreach and assertively building relationships. Masculine sales strategies are focused on "doing" and achieving, and are moulded by logic and reason. In contrast, feminine sales approaches are more intuitive, oriented towards receiving and allowing, and characterised by "being".

Masculine sales approaches are structured and organised and rely on facts and figures, whereas the feminine approach may never look the same way twice for each sale and may rely more on emotions. Feminine-led sales is not necessarily better than masculine-led sales. If you swing too far one way, you can find yourself in inaction and relying on "luck". If you swing too far the other way, you can end up in burn out from too much "doing".

A common problem I see many coaches struggle with is learning how to sell in a way that feels authentic to them. We often lack good examples of sales approaches that feel aligned for us.

Picture a typical sales leader in your mind. Someone who crushes their sales quota every quarter and was seemingly born to sell. Is the person you're picturing a man? I wouldn't be surprised if it is. Yet a study found that on average, women in sales outperform their male counterparts when it comes to making quota, with eighty-six percent of women making quota compared to seventy-eight percent of men.

Of course, masculine *and* feminine energy exist in men, women and non-binary people. But the research shows that typically women are naturally stronger salespeople. This is because we are more likely to focus on building strong rela-tionships and earning clients' trust, are proactive listeners so we get to the root of the situation, have intuition and listen to our gut feelings, and see the complexities and dig deeper to find the best solution for clients.

While high-performing saleswomen are more likely to place emphasis on connection, shaping solutions, and collaboration, high-performing men rely more on improving and driving outcomes, "netting it out", and relying on logic to land the deal. I believe a balance of the feminine and masculine approaches to selling is needed for you to truly access your full income potential. You might be swinging too far one way right now and it's blocking your ability to attract new clients.

For me personally, balancing the masculine and feminine in our sales approach looks like this.

Masculine: Having booking systems and automations in place, diving into the detail of the client's situation to determine a likely number-based outcome, and having a follow-up system to reach back out to warm leads.

Feminine: Listening to my intuition regarding whether a client is a good fit or not, inviting them to check in with their intuition before making a decision, and focusing on building relationships and rapport.

Launching as a marketing strategy can feel more masculine, whereas evergreen is more feminine. However, you still need a balance of masculine and feminine approaches for evergreen marketing to work.

FOMO, Scarcity and Deadline Tactics

I used to rely on scarcity and unnecessary deadlines to incentivise clients to invest in my group coaching program. I thought it was a necessary evil to help more people. That was, until a few big problems came to light.

When you rely on Fear of Missing Out (FOMO) tactics such as scarcity and deadlines to make people buy high-ticket coaching programs, you run the risk of having more unhappy clients who aren't getting results because they joined before they felt ready to commit and do the work. In other words, their reason for investing was because they were about to miss out on something, rather than feeling ready to fully commit to the result they were signing up to create with your help.

FOMO tactics can also lead to increased refund rates because clients bought on "scarcity" rather than real desire, and then get Buyer's Remorse soon afterwards and regret their decision. I totally get why you might think you can't sell group programs without a launch deadline. It's probably what we've been conditioned to believe by the marketing gurus out there that teach these tactics. But if learning to sell without the need for FOMO meant your client results increased and your refund requests declined, would you be open to learning how?

I used to believe I had to recreate my offer again and again by adding bonuses like an extra one-to-one call with me for a limited time only, just to incentivise people to say Yes by a certain deadline. But it never really felt authentic, and recreating the offer every month just to create demand was exhausting and not sustainable. It also trains your audience to wait for the next juicy offer from you before finally saying yes. You can probably think of at least one brand you don't purchase from until they have a sale on.

Do you want that for your group coaching program or master-mind? I personally don't want my audience waiting for me to come out with a fancy new discount or a fancy new offer just to make them say yes to themselves. Occasionally, you will make a genuine change in the offer and pricing, but unless it's genuine, re-creating your offer to generate fake urgency will only work for so long.

Instead, to create genuine urgency and reason to invest, you have to appeal to people's inner sense of urgency. What does that mean exactly? The answer lies in identifying why working with you is a *now* thing for that particular person. Why is this the perfect time for them to make a change?

Sometimes this requires you to highlight the pain or struggle they are putting up with by not saying yes to themselves. What pain are they in right now, or what opportunity and benefit are they missing out on by staying where they are and not taking action?

One of my clients works with entrepreneurs and their energy. She helps them uplevel who they are being and the frequency they are operating at, so they can call in more opportunities and more advanced or aligned clients. By doing the energy and transformation work with her, her clients are able to attract and land clients and contracts worth $100,000 or more. But when I caught up with her on a one-to-one call, she shared with me that of the last four sales conversations she'd had, all four of those potential clients had pushed off working with her until the future.

I asked her if she'd highlighted what they were saying No to by postponing the decision to work with her. In other words, a client could be saying No to signing four $100,000 clients in the next twelve months and therefore be missing out on an income of $400,000.

To appeal to your potential client's inner sense of urgency, look for the downside and upside of them saying Yes or No to taking action. Don't be afraid to highlight this to them from a place of love, knowing that you have their best interests at heart. And if they still don't want to invest right there and then, at least you know they're making that decision having taken both the upside and downside into account.

The second piece to identifying someone's inner sense of urgency is to ask them why they would want to wait. Maybe they have a legitimate reason, like wanting to take a vacation or finish something else first. And if they do, and they're still a Yes to working with you, great! Take a deposit and book them in for when they're ready to work with you in a few months' time. Just because you're ready to sell something to them, doesn't mean they're ready to buy from you. Your potential client might be a 'Yes' buying from you in the future, just not right now.

People really like being able to invest in their future selves. Think about how you feel when you sign yourself up and pay for something you believe is going to improve your life in some way, such as a personal trainer or a new qualification. I usually feel pretty darn happy with myself and begin to work forward to the transformation happening.

But what if you feel like you're doing all the right things in your sales conversations, yet they're still not converting as well as you want them to?

I have a checklist for you, my friend, to help you identify where your gap(s) might be when it comes to conversion. Use the checklist below to rate yourself on a scale of one to ten (where ten is nailing it and one signifies a gap for you) and see where your biggest opportunities are for improvement in your mastery of sales conversion.

1. Are the people getting on the calls with you the right people in the first place – are they qualified leads?
You might not be clear on what a qualified lead looks like for you. Start by identifying what characteristics a great ideal client has. For example, what stage in their journey are they at? What might they have tried before? Are they ready to make a change or just window shopping for details?
Once you have these key characteristics clear, update your application and pre-call process to ensure you're speaking to the people you can truly help most.

2. Is the offer right for them? Are you selling the right thing to the right person, or does your ideal client or offer need to change a little?

3. Is your articulation of the offer strong enough to convey the value, i.e., do you describe the outcome of

the program in a way that connects with their current desires/problems?

4. Are you people-pleasing or leading in the conversation? Leading looks like you challenging their thinking (with love), and sharing your perspective on their problem.

5. Do you feel certain about your offer, the process you take people through and the outcome you'll help them achieve? Do you show that certainty with your language, or do doubts about your offer and ability to help people hold you back?

6. Is it clear why they'd work with you over others? Perhaps you have some things in common, a similar background story or have achieved something similar to what they want. Are you building rapport on the call?

7. Do you shed light on the gap between where they are now and where they want to be? Or does carrying on the way they are and doing things on their own still seem like a viable option by the end of the conversation?

8. If they don't make a decision on the call, do you clarify what's holding them back from a yes? Do you hold non-judgemental space for them to share their concerns, worries, fears and questions? If they need time to think, do you lovingly ask, "What do you need

to think about?"... and do you book a follow-up call if they need it in a few days?

9. Are you too attached to the outcome? On a scale of "I couldn't give a monkey's because another lead will show up tomorrow" (one) to "I really want this sale" (ten) where do you sit out of ten? Somewhere around five to seven is often a good place to be. You want to care, but not so much that it comes across as desperate.

Mastering sales conversations is a process and if you faceplant your first ten to twenty calls, don't worry, you're not doomed. Just keep going in the name of developing this skill set for yourself and you will absolutely get there. I used to truly suck at sales and now it's something I'm pretty great at. I didn't do any specific sales training courses and simply learned through observation and practice. It took fifteen sales calls to land my first Yes, so if you're in the same place right now, keep going!

Once you learn how to sell yourself in the form of a group coaching offer, you can truly sell anything because there's nothing like the mindset gremlins that come up when you're in the business of selling your own expertise. The imposter syndrome, self-doubt and mind monkeys are the absolute worst when you're selling your own value. Selling anything else in the future will be hilariously easy in comparison. Stick with it and you'll thank your former self for gifting yourself the art of selling.

Every single one of the pennies that made up the million pounds in cash I had made in my business before turning thirty was a penny I had personally asked for in a sales conversation in some capacity, whether on a zoom call, a direct message conversation or on a sales page for a low-cost course. I'm wildly proud of that and it makes me feel pretty unstoppable. The same empowered feeling is completely available to you too.

9

MILLION DOLLAR EVERGREEN FUNNEL

AFTER A LONG, unhappy day at work, I found myself watching a free training on my phone after clicking on a Facebook Ad. The speaker was talking about the opportunity to make money online as a coach. It wasn't hugely relevant to me at the time since I was still in my job at McKinsey, so I never took her up on her offer of a free call, but I stayed in that coach's world for two and a half years until finally investing to work with her.

That was back in 2015. What I'd fallen across was an evergreen webinar funnel.

The question is, do evergreen webinars still work now, at least eight years later? Online marketing moves fast, so can something as retro as an evergreen webinar still have a place in your marketing strategy? I've got a lot of thoughts on this and I'm about to drop some serious knowledge on you, so buckle up.

No idea what a webinar is?

Chances are, if you've consumed any kind of online marketing, you've ended up watching a webinar at some point, whether you knew that's what it was or not. A webinar is simply a video (live or recorded) in which the speaker talks about the problem their ideal customer is experiencing. (Ideally, you as the viewer are their ideal customer.) They talk about how their approach solves this problem, and they share the details of their offer or at least a next step for you to take if you're interested in what they have to sell. It's essentially a long-form sales pitch that can be delivered to the masses because it's accessible online at any time.

In my opinion, the whole point of marketing is to take a cold lead and walk them through the process of deciding whether they want to buy your thing or not. That's it. You want to help them figure out if they're the right fit for your program and, ultimately, make a purchase.

Most entrepreneurs have no idea that their marketing is meant to take people down the buyer decision-making process, which is why you see a lot of coaches throwing spaghetti at the wall with their marketing. They have no idea how their marketing content is meant to take somebody from "cold" to "sold". This leaves them with no idea why their marketing strategies aren't working. When their marketing does work, it feels kind of random, so when their marketing stops working, they don't know how to fix it.

What is the buyer decision-making process exactly?

When a wonderful human enters your online world for the first time, they bring with them a certain set of beliefs about you, what you're offering and about themselves. On the other hand, a human who has just purchased from you has a different set of beliefs. Bridging the gap between these two sets of beliefs makes up the buyer decision-making process. It's essentially a thought process that your ideal client has to go down from being a cold, new lead in your world to making a buying decision.

This process could take a few days, a few months, or sometimes years. I've had people binge-watch my livestreams, read all my social media content and watch my evergreen webinar in just a few days and then sign up to work with me. My content is specifically designed to take the right people down the buyer decision-making process, and to repel the ones who aren't the best people for me to help. It's both an art and a science.

What methods are available to you for taking a lead down that buyer decision-making process? And is a webinar really the best option?

Option one is your written social media content. But will your potential client see all the bits of content they need to see before purchasing? Potentially not unless they have the time to binge-read everything. They will read your content over time, of course, but you often have to rely on people seeing your content repeatedly for them to have all of those questions answered and be able to finally say, "Yes, I'm going to sign up." Relying on content alone also requires you to write a huge amount of content.

Your second option might be a multi-day challenge launch in which you deliver nuggets of valuable training every day for three to five days and then invite people to purchase from you. However, do you want to launch every few months to drive revenue in your business? Probably not if you've read the previous chapters.

Your third option is to have long sales conversations over the phone or Zoom, which is hugely time-consuming.

When you look outside the online space, you will typically see a fairly long sales lead time before a purchase is made for a high-ticket item. The sales team or the CEO spends time building various relationships with people who eventually become clients. When purchasing a car or house, you'll take time to do your research and consider a few options.

There's a lot of time investment required from you as the entrepreneur if you're going to rely on the third option.

A long sales page is your fourth option, but these don't generally convert well for high-ticket investments without another touch point with the potential new client.

We generated over $400,000 in sales into one of my group coaching programs before writing a sales page for the program. The most important thing to focus on is understanding your ideal buyer inside out and that requires conversations with people, rather than guesswork that leads to copy which doesn't convert.

A sales page is best when the potential buyer is right at the end of their buyer decision-making process and they've probably already received enough information from you elsewhere to know it's worth them checking out the sales page.

Sales pages aren't hugely useful for taking people down the buyer decision-making process from start to finish. You rarely get a cold lead land on your sales page who then invests a high-ticket amount with you right away. It can happen but only in a small minority of instances. Frankly, I don't want the success of my business to be reliant on a small minority of instances.

Your fifth option, therefore, is a well-crafted webinar, in which you can take a cold lead down that buyer decision-making process within thirty to sixty minutes by giving them everything they need to be able to decide if it's the right thing for them or not.

But the thing is, most webinars really suck. When you see people say that webinars don't convert, question the source of that information. Is it because they've tried and a webinar didn't work for them specifically, and now they believe it doesn't work for anyone?

A lot of the old bro-marketing approaches to webinars really suck, especially if you're selling to a predominantly female audience. The fake scarcity and deadlines also do not work when you're running them evergreen. The market increasingly sees right through these shallow tactics of countdown timers that don't mean anything.

Not all webinars are created equal. And this is why I crafted my own process for taking somebody down the buyer decision-making process within a webinar storyline. Using sales psychology and coaching approaches in the webinar itself is a game changer. I teach this method to my clients, of course, who have people quoting the webinar back to them and signing up to their programs with ease because it landed so well in their minds.

So webinars are the fifth option and are by far the most effective way to take a lead from cold to sold in a short amount of time. At the very least, if a new lead watches a part of the video, they'll know if you're relevant to them or not. If you are, they'll continue consuming your content online and via email until they eventually buy when the timing is right for them.

But here's the thing: only one to three percent of your audience is actually ready to buy at any given time. These are the people who are aware of their problem and are actively searching for a solution. Another thirty-seven percent are aware of their problem, but they're not sure what solution they need yet. The remaining sixty percent? They don't even know they have a problem.

So, how do you use evergreen webinars to sell your high-ticket group coaching program to that tiny three percent of ready buyers? The answer is to guide them down the buyer decision-making process; help them to figure out if your program is right for them and then to make a buying decision.

Here's something else to keep in mind: that cohort of one to three percent ready buyers is constantly changing. The people who were ready to buy last month might not be the same people who are ready this month or even this week. This means you've always got to bring new leads into your marketing funnel and guide them through the buyer decision-making process.

People typically buy within a few days or weeks of being ready to. There is now a new set of people in that three percent the following month. When you rely on launching and closing the doors to your program in between launches, you miss out on the three percent of people that become ready to buy in the following months.

When you have an evergreen funnel in your business, you are able to sell to that three percent of people every month, rather than just the month you decide to launch. The evergreen funnel and the simple marketing ecosystem of touchpoints you have created help to take the other thirty-seven percent of your market who are problem-aware and becoming solution-aware down that buyer decision-making process and help them to become ready to invest in the following months.

Of the clients we interviewed, every one of them consumed at least three pieces of long-form content from me before deciding to purchase. These pieces of content were either my podcast (Grow To CEO), my livestreams on Facebook or Instagram, or my evergreen webinar. In fact, over 90% of the clients we interviewed had watched the evergreen webinar. Instead of relying on your leads to consume and piece together all the bits of social media content they need to be taken down the buyer decision-making process, why not deliver it all to them succinctly in one pre-recorded training that takes less than an hour to consume?

It's no secret that a free webinar has an invitation to take the next step and buy. Some people will watch your webinar as part of their active buying experience with you, knowing that they are going to be able to find out more about working with you and get a feel of who you are from consuming that short training from you. Equally, someone who is willing to sit through a training to help find the solution to their problem is typically in enough of a state of pain or heightened desire for a different result in their life, that they're willing to invest that time in finding the solution.

Your webinar is a lead magnet. It attracts either buyers who are shopping around and ready to invest pretty darn soon (the three percent) or buyers who are in the thirty-seven percent and aware of their pain so are actively looking for a solution and are willing to invest time to watch something that will educate them on that solution. In doing so, this latter type of person moves from being in the thirty-seven percent to the three percent.

The evergreen webinar funnel we use in my business was first launched in April 2021 and alone has delivered over USD $1.3M in the eighteen months since. A webinar is a deeply powerful marketing tool in your business when done well and an asset that will deliver results to you for years.

When you have a refined evergreen webinar funnel in place, you can expect to have applications to work with you drop in every week. Just like my client Kathryn who woke up to new applications in her inbox almost every morning within a month of launching her funnel. She signed seven new high-ticket clients from just $3,000 in Ad spend within six weeks of launching her new evergreen webinar funnel. She experienced a sixty percent conversion rate on her sales calls because her leads were taken so far down the buyer decision-making process in the webinar that it made the sales conversation really easy.

With consistent leads like this coming in, any sense of scarcity and pressure to make the sale disappears because you know there are always new potential clients coming into your world.

Bottom line: evergreen webinars are a powerful tool for guiding leads through the decision-making process in under an hour, and I've yet to find an equally efficient way of achieving the same outcome in less time.

Are you addicted to launching?

If you've done a few launches and created some success that way, and are now looking to go evergreen, you might have fallen into the trap of feeling that you just need "one more launch" before you can go evergreen. A coach who has gener-ated multi-seven-figures from launching over the years shared with me that she always had a reason to need to do just one more launch before doing the thing she actually wanted to do. There was always a tax bill to pay, a business debt to pay, or she was going to close the program so she felt she might as well do one last push for sales. It is really easy to fall into that thinking loop because it all feels so logical at the time. But when the dust settles after the launch and the cash injection begins to run out, you find yourself back in the same need to launch to keep the business going.

The pattern repeats again and again until you gain conscious awareness of it and decide to do things differently. Often, it takes a bad launch to force a coach in this situation to become serious about going evergreen, so they at least have a cushion of consistent sales coming in on top of their launches.

The other thing about big launches, or launching in general, is that they're really good for your ego. Your ego really enjoys the idea of you having a $50K or even $500k launch. Big launches can give you kudos: people begin to know you as somebody who has successful launches.

You can become attached to the identity of being a multi-six or seven-figure launcher. Unhooking yourself from that and beginning to grow your business in a more sustainable way can bring up a great deal of internal resistance, especially as your brain has learnt that launching leads to success. Doing anything different feels incredibly risky and destabilising.

As a launch-based coach, you most likely think and speak in "Launch", as if it's a language. When you come to sell an offer, you think about when you're going to close the cart, what bonuses you're offering, how many emails you need, and so on.

But that's not the language of "Evergreen" – they're different languages. That's not to say it's really complicated to go from Launching to Evergreen. There are also many people out there who use both really successfully. It's a case of learning a new but similar language. In Portugal, a large proportion of expats are Brazilians. They speak Brazilian Portuguese which is similar to the European Portuguese language but is pronounced very differently, so they have to relearn their own language because it's "same-same but different" from the local Portuguese. Learning Evergreen as a Launcher is similar to learning European Portuguese as a Brazilian.

In my experience, the launch-based coaching crowd feel as if they thrive on the pressure of a launch. When it comes to running a stable, simple, heavily systemised business that's easy to run on a day-to-day basis, it feels boring compared to the common high-stakes, high-pressure, slightly terrifying grit-your-teeth launch situation that they're very used to, but they're also not really enjoying anymore.

Sometimes this launch addiction is led by the unconscious belief that you've got to work hard to make money so only the hard work of a launch makes you deserving of more money. There's nothing better than a stressful launch with many moving pieces to make you feel as though you've worked hard enough to deserve the money you make from it.

Another common reason for the addiction to launching is driven by a bad experience of giving evergreen marketing a try and it not working. One bad experience can be enough to put some coaches off trying again, but if you had one bad date, would you swear off dating ever again? That simply wouldn't make sense.

When done well, an evergreen marketing strategy can be far more profitable than launching. Great launches require extra resources and investment such as more team members and more Ad spend. There's no guarantee of these investments paying off in a launch, though. On the other hand, running an evergreen business often means your costs are the same every month and your team become super efficient and sharp, so there's less waste, rework and over-spending.

If you continue to be addicted to launches, you're saying yes to less profitability, to more work, to potentially declining results and to unpredictable results in your launches. The good news is that if you can handle complicated launches with many moving pieces, setting up an evergreen marketing strategy will be a piece of cake for you.

How fast can you go evergreen?

You may have heard that a new evergreen webinar funnel can take three to six months to fully optimise and to generate a strong profit. I both agree and disagree with this. You can patiently play the long game, knowing that you're optimising an asset that can generate millions for you over time, while also using shorter-term tactics to generate results within a few weeks and months.

I've personally created entire evergreen webinar funnels in one rainy weekend. You can make this as complicated and as difficult as you want it to be… or you can decide to make it easy.

Many of my clients will initially want to make a mountain out of a molehill with their evergreen funnels but that only delays their results. I love challenging the talented women I work with to simply "get it done" and to stop blocking their results with procrastination. Just like Melanie who got her Direct

Messaging sales funnel built in one week and was generating new sales within the first few weeks of us working together.

In answer to the question of how fast you can go evergreen, I believe you can have your cake and eat it with evergreen sales – when you know the short-term tactics you can implement alongside your longer-term strategies.

PART 4

AUDIENCE

10

ATTRACTING AN AUDIENCE OF BUYERS

I USED to use the word "audience" to describe the group of people who might buy from me in the future. And to be honest, it felt weird to use that word from the start.

An audience watches someone on stage but rarely engages. They purchase tickets, but they rarely interact with the person on stage, unless it's a pantomime of course, but that's not the vibe here. Having an "audience" puts you on a pedestal as the coach and business owner. It suggests there's just a one-way conversation between you and them, rather than a back and forth connection.

I then used the words "leads" and "prospects" because a talented marketer I knew used those words too. But those words, although technically correct in the world of marketing, made it feel like I was only interested in people if they were going to buy from me. The words felt "bro-markety" and impersonal.

If you want to create a two-way communication with the people who may buy from you in the future, and you don't want to reduce those people to mere numbers, what's the alternative way of naming and viewing your potential future clients? It may sound obvious, but the word "community" does a far better job of describing the people you're cultivating around your business who may buy from you in the future.

Despite what you may have been taught about being ever-green, I still believe there's a place for organic community building in your business, rather than relying solely on an Ad that goes to an evergreen funnel. (However, we'll touch on Ads later and I'll share how I regularly turn $3,000 of Ad spend into $75,000 cash months, and how you can too.) A business with a community will stand the test of time. It will still be here in decades to come if you want it to. Building an organic community also hedges against the risk of your Ad account being shut down. At the later stages of business, your job as the CEO and leader of the company is as much about managing and hedging against risk, as it is about growth.

So how do you build a large enough community in your business to fuel its growth, without reducing people to mere numbers? The first shift to make is an internal one and requires you to adopt two new "identities": let's call them the *community leader* and the *content creator*. As a community leader, you're bringing people together, connecting them through common values and aspirations, and hosting a space for them to connect.

You can build a community on any social media platform, whether it's YouTube, Instagram, a podcast or even TikTok.

There is no right or wrong platform to use. Instead, it is simply a case of choosing one you enjoy most and deciding to truly master it, rather than jumping from one to another.

If you're just starting out in your business and are new to leading a community, perhaps sharing content or doing a livestream to drop some value bombs on your potential future clients feels terrifying right now. If that is the case, simply start by building a small Facebook group. This is the exact move I made at the start of my business. It helped me adopt the identity of community leader and gave me a safe space to go live in without completely wetting my pants about it.

The second identity shift is about becoming a content creator. As an online entrepreneur, content creation is like a muscle you build over time. Posting content to your platforms almost every day becomes a baseline habit.

When I first started my business, I committed to posting something to Instagram and Facebook every single day without fail and I kept that habit for over eighteen months. I'm not saying you have to post every day, although of course that will naturally increase the number of times your community may see something valuable from you. Instead, the act of committing to posting every day was the transformation for me.

It signalled to my community and to me that I'm reliable, that I'm all in on this business, and that I'm here for them. At a time when I was doubting myself and whether I had "what it takes" to make the business successful, that one act of commitment compounded over time made all the difference to my brain in building belief in myself. Now when I post content online, I don't really think about it and it's just a baseline habit in the business.

Choose the amount of content you want to commit to creating. It might be three or five posts a week. Either way, make the decision and commit to a consistent follow-through and it'll do your self-belief and self-trust a world of good, especially if you're in need of some of that right now!

However, do not just post online in the form of inspirational quotes or mindless content purely so you can tick the box. Your content has a purpose, and that purpose is to start conversations. Conversations lead to the two-way communication you need for community building and, of course, conversations also lead to sales because sales is a contact sport.

At the awards night for the National Women's Business Awards in the UK, which I walked away from with the Young Business Woman Of The Year Award (yay!), I sat next to someone who said something to me that really got my goat.

It was clear she had concluded that I was an influencer and my job was to post on social media. *Nope!* At the time, I ran training and consulting programs with a team of two full-time and three part-time team members.

I now run a business that uses social media for marketing and sales. Posting to social media does not make you an influencer. You run a business. As CEO, I deal with the sh*t, make the hard decisions, invest the money, take the risks, and have the difficult conversations that most people would rather shy away from. Some weeks I really earn my money as CEO.

You are the same. Posting on social media does not make you an influencer. Even though your friends and family may see it that way, don't let that stop you showing up for your business and using the incredible and free social media tools that are at your fingertips. I've got nothing against influencers. I'm not here to throw shade at other businesses and their eye for design is far better than mine ever will be.

One of the biggest challenges that holds coaches back from being able to genuinely evergreen and scale their group coaching program to seven-plus figures, and sign one to three (or more) clients a week, is the pace and volume of potential new clients entering their world every day. If your community isn't growing and being taken down the buyer decision-making process by your evergreen marketing, then the sales into your program simply won't appear.

So how do you grow your community every day, even if it's just by three more people? Having been a strategy consultant for a while, I can't help but think in threes so of course I have a three-pronged approach to growing your community: Organic, Partnership and Paid.

Organic traffic is anything you do for free to grow your online community. Instead of investing money in the form of Ads, you're mainly investing your time.

Partnership traffic is about leveraging other people's audiences to help you connect with more of the right people and grow your own community. If you're starting from scratch without any online community like I did, leveraging other people's audiences is the best and fastest way to grow your own audience for free.

Partnership traffic strategies include:

- Adding value to other people's Facebook groups or communities
- Delivering guest trainings in other people's paid and free communities or programs
- Guesting on other people's podcasts
- Building a referral network

And many more.

Your third option is of course Paid traffic via Facebook/Instagram, YouTube, Google Ads or TikTok.

Community building requires you to spend either time or money. Depending on how quickly you want to be able to grow and how much of each resource you have, you get to choose which of the three levers you pull. I don't recommend trying to pull all the levers at the same time at the very start, unless you have a big budget and team, and you don't require sleep any time soon.

The simplest, easiest way to approach community building is to master one or two approaches at a time until it's working and you can systemise and hand over that approach.

Whichever traffic sources you use, all roads lead to your funnel. Instead of sending people in lots of different directions, send them all to one place and let that funnel do the heavy lifting for you by turning your new cold leads into clients. The simplicity in this approach is freeing.

11

BIG RESULTS, SMALL AUDIENCE

MY APPROACH to evergreen marketing is different from what you may have come across before. Traditionally, the word evergreen in the context of marketing has been used to sell low-ticket offers to generate passive income. However, this way of doing evergreen lacks intimacy and requires a massive audience to scale. This means it's not an easy or fast way to grow your coaching business. The fastest and easiest way to grow your business is by crafting a high-ticket evergreen group coaching program and selling it via an evergreen funnel (as you now know!)... but not the traditional evergreen funnel.

Firstly, this evergreen funnel doesn't require a sales page. Instead, we have conversations via direct messages (sometimes Zoom) that lead to sales. In fact, we generated $400K in sales before we even set up a sales page for the Freedom Accelerator, and even now, most of our clients sign up for our program without ever seeing the sales page.

Think about the compounding benefits of having conversations with your ideal prospects. You build genuine connections with your community, and that's how you scale a business that stands the test of time. As one of my recent new clients said, "I'm loving every step of this funnel experience I've been down towards you and can't wait to have my own." By default, you're getting to know your people inside and out. You can (and should) use this insight to optimise your offers and marketing assets for conversions.

Being evergreen doesn't need to mean everything happens automatically. Yes, there is a solid foundation of automation supporting you and creating spaciousness in so many activities, such as lead generation, taking leads down the buyer decision-making process, and program onboarding. But when you have automation giving you space, you can inject intimacy in the right places of your funnel with precision. High-ticket investments often require a level of intimacy before the sale happens, and that's why we lead with conversations rather than a sales page.

Maybe the only people you're connected with on social media are your former colleagues or old friends. In that case, you can't play the "I've got a big audience" card in your lead generation strategy. But you can turn this perceived weakness into a strength by playing the intimacy card in your marketing instead. Even though you might feel like the small size of your online community is a limitation to your business, it's actually a strength when you realise you can feasibly connect with a smaller group of people online.

The intimacy card is when you treat each person in your community as an individual and connect with them one to one. The easiest way to do this is through Direct Message (DM) on social media, but if you're at the very beginning of your business journey, you can of course go deeper and jump on fifteen- or thirty-minute calls with as many people as possible to learn more about them, and to offer them a free assessment or coaching session.

I used the DM approach to get fully booked with one-to-one clients within eight weeks at the beginning of my business and we've continued to use them since to build intimacy and trust and to therefore increase sales overall.

Whenever I mention selling in DMs to a fellow online entrepreneur, they assume I'm talking about sending cold pitch DMs to one hundred people a day, knowing that one poor soul out of that hundred will be desperate enough to reply. That is not it. I enjoy receiving cold DM pitches as little as the next person. In fact, cold DMs in general feel somewhat invasive.

I love to use a combination of permission-based DMs and inbound DMs.

A permission-based DM is when the lead has already entered your world in some way and shown some interest in what you have to offer, so now it's a case of you working out if you can truly help them. For example, a lead may come into your free Facebook group, connect with you on LinkedIn, sign up to your free webinar funnel, follow you on Instagram or comment on a social media post that shows they want the details of your offer.

If you host an event one evening at which you're speaking to a small group of people, and some people show up who you don't know, you are likely to head over and get to know them. The same principle applies when people enter your corners of the internet and you send them a DM. You're simply welcoming them in and finding out how you might be able to help them.

This action of initiating a permission-based conversation also helps your audience feel comfortable messaging you in the future when they're ready to learn more, which supports the second part of the DM strategy I love: Inbound DMs.

Our inbound DM strategy has led us to receive between two and seven, and sometimes more, leads per day into our social media inboxes from people inquiring about the details of a program.

When the conversation is initiated by the potential customer themselves, the conversation is wildly different and so much easier for you as the person making the sale. You are sorting through and qualifying the leads, rather than selling to them. Once you know they are someone you can help and it sounds like it would be a great fit for them, that's when you share the invitation to purchase and all the other details they might need.

One of the reasons we generated $900,000 USD in cash into the business in 2022 from only $27,900 in Ad spend and fewer than nine thousand people in our Instagram community (that's a thirty-two times return on our Ad spend investment with no other PR or external marketing investment) is because of the relationships and conversations we built via DMs.

A person is far more likely to buy from someone they feel they can trust and who cares enough about that person to have a quick conversation that helps them make a buying decision.

If you're waiting for someone to land on the sales page for your program and buy it out of the blue, you could be waiting a very long time. The Tony Robbinses and Brendon Burchards of the world may be able to do this but their online communities are massive and their brands have been around a long time. They have more trust built in their communities so it's much easier for someone to buy a high-ticket offer from them without needing a conversation to help them make a decision. A low-ticket purchase of less than $2,000, depending on the niche, may not need a conversation. But as your group program is probably more than that, you're in a world where having more conversations leads to more conversions.

I'm not Tony Robbins, and chances are, you're not either. So instead of the "Big Audience Size" Card, we're playing the "Intimacy" Card and here's how you can overcome the blocks that might be holding you back from doing that right now.

But does all this DM action lead you to live in your social media inboxes forever? I asked the same question a few months after getting fully booked with private clients and moving into selling a group coaching program. I was spending two to three hours a day messaging people, which was unsustainable while also running the business and supporting clients.

I took what felt like a wild leap at the time and hired a recent university graduate with zero sales experience and trained her on my approach and scripts. I was clear with her that I had no idea if this role in my business would be viable and we agreed to test it out together for ninety days.

Within the first thirty days, she nurtured a lead who became a $15,000 client. There was no way I would have signed that client without the work done by my new DM assistant. I've had a DM assistant in my business ever since and my clients love having this kind of support too. My DM assistant and I tag-team conversations and she develops and follows flexible scripts using her intuition and curiosity. I love this role in a coaching business because it's so clearly income-generating when done well; in a small business, every team member must be adding genuine value.

If you want big results when you still only have a small online community, don't hide behind the screen. Instead, be willing to show you really care and connect with the humans on the other side of the screen. Find ways to help them and you won't wonder where your next client will come from ever again. In a world where Artificial Intelligence is quickly becoming a key part of the marketing, sales and delivery journeys for our clients, intimacy will be rare. I strongly believe that those who maintain intimacy with their audience will maintain their brand trust and business growth.

12

TURNING $3K INTO $75K A MONTH

WOULD you spend $3,000 knowing it would generate $75,000 back for you per month? That's probably a silly question. Your answer is almost certainly, *"Yes!"*

First, some context. Are we talking about revenue or profit, cash received or sales value? And what exactly does the money get spent on to create that outcome?

I love seeing and understanding the inside of other people's businesses that are further on than mine so I can see what's possible and understand where I might have some gaps right now. I'm incredibly transparent with my business numbers because it allows you to see what's possible for you, and it makes what I'm sharing feel more tangible. Your numbers will probably be different and I'm not making any guarantees other than that I'll always share the real numbers with you.

The $3,000 was in fact $2,300 per month on average in 2022 if we were to be precise. Rounding to $3,000 makes the numbers simpler to work with and this is how much we would typically spend in a month we actually ran Ads. The money was spent on Facebook and Instagram Ads. The $75,000 was the average amount of cash received into the business on a monthly basis. We spent just under $28,000 on Ads for the entirety of 2022 and we brought in $900,000 in cash in that same year. In other words, that was a thirty-two times return on ad spend, where investing $1 led to generating $32 back.

It's not just me doing this. I have countless examples of clients doing the same, such as repeatedly turning $500 Ad spend into $5,000 sales and spending £225 to acquire a new £2,500 client every week. These are real numbers and the crazy thing is, both of these sets of numbers come from funnels that are only a few months old and haven't been thoroughly optimised. These funnels will generate even more profitability in the future for these clients.

It's these kinds of things that get me ridiculously excited for clients because we can both see how empowering it is to have an automated funnel that brings life-changing results into their business that will only ever stack and increase over time. Even though it might be a chunk of work up front to get the system running, the juice is completely worth the squeeze. It makes me hugely passionate about helping more entrepreneurs create incredibly powerful evergreen funnels.

There are real humans on the other side of these numbers and these funnels bring amazing new clients to work with. I would never want to dehumanise the evergreen marketing experience by talking about numbers all the time. In fact, using intimacy in your marketing (see the previous chapter) will put faces to numbers and make the figures even more meaningful. At the same time, it's really important that you understand your numbers and that you know what is and isn't driving growth, so you know where to put the money to grow.

Of course, part of our story is that we'd invested in the business in the years previously which led to further revenue growth in 2022, but we still had a very small audience at the time. This is worth highlighting because coaches often tell me they've sworn off pursuing an evergreen marketing strategy until their audience is a lot larger, but this couldn't be further from the truth of what is possible.

My clients and I have grown businesses on evergreen from tiny audiences. You absolutely can generate sales every week and every month if you're a newer business. This approach keeps you afloat and generates momentum much faster than depending on a launch every few months and therefore limiting your ability to generate income outside of a launch. The latter can be lethal to a new business.

Our level of return on Ad spend is very different from the general online marketing ethos that suggests you should spend between ten and twenty percent of your revenue on Ads and expect to receive $5-10 per $1 spent. We create results that smash industry standards out of the park because of a few things I've learned over the years.

The first factor of our success is that we sell higher ticket offers, because the results we support clients to create are hugely valuable. Identify exactly what hugely valuable result you help your high-ticket clients create.

The second key to your success is to optimise your funnel over time so it generates better and better results when you know exactly what to look for. This is one of the things I love about running an evergreen business: you can really drive up your profit margin when you make strategic changes and test new things incrementally. This is the magical compound effect of evergreen marketing. Instead of creating quick cash injections in a launch with lots of extra effort and then making very few sales for a few months, an evergreen approach means your income stacks month on month, as long as you continue to use the process.

When you compare this to a launch where your costs often spike due to hiring extra team support, investing more in Ads and creating more marketing assets, with a lot more risk because you don't know how much the launch is going to pay off, you can see why it's easier to build a stable business on evergreen. You can even be left in the red with a launch if it doesn't quite go to plan.

What's better than spending $3K on Ads for a launch and getting $75K back in that launch? It's being able to do that every month, minus the extra launch effort.

The third reason we're able to create these profitable results is down to the retargeting that we have in place. Gone are the days when you can just whip up an evergreen webinar funnel and expect a large number of people to sign up instantly. That used to be the case in 2015, but not any more.

There is a larger amount of mistrust and scepticism in the online space today and this requires more nurturing, time and intimacy to overcome. This means you have to show up a few more times in front of your potential future clients to build more trust and help them understand how you can help them.

You are likely to convert around one percent of your leads in the first thirty days, and to increase that overall conversion rate in the long run, use additional points of contact such as emails, organic content, content-based Ads, direct messages and/or a private community such as a Facebook or Telegram group. You probably won't need all of these but adding a few retargeting strategies will have a huge impact on your results.

The fourth ingredient is intangible and the hardest thing to do, but is often the most important. It is to believe that evergreen marketing is going to work for you. I see so many coaches sabotage things because they give up too soon, switch focus and decide prematurely it's not working fast enough. They give in to their shiny object syndrome and give up five minutes before the miracle.

To stop yourself from throwing away all your efforts as you venture down the evergreen route, notice all the ways in which the system is working already. There will be kinks and opportunities for optimisation, for sure, but that doesn't need to stop you from generating results within the first few months. Recognise that you're currently on the road to leveraging the magical compound effect of continuous improvement. In another four to six months, you will be in a wildly different place and generating supernormal profits because you stayed the course while other people gave up.

Some people will turn Ads off because they don't know what to look for in the data. They don't realise the ads are creating results for them. This is why I look at my clients' stats with them to equip them with the understanding they need to make great decisions long after we finish working together. There's nothing more empowering than being able to make game-changing strategic decisions for your business based on understanding your data.

MUST you run Ads to go evergreen with your group coaching program?

Most coaches believe you have to run Facebook or Instagram Ads to sell your group coaching programs using an evergreen marketing strategy in order to enrol new clients into your programs every week and month. This puts a lot of coaches off from going evergreen because they fear spending money on Ads, don't know how to use them, or worry that it won't work.

The belief that you must run Ads for an evergreen marketing strategy simply isn't true. I can see why you might think that though. You see so many Ads on your feed from coaches and you also hear people preaching about how you must run Ads to grow your audience and scale your business.

Facebook and Instagram Ads help you grow your audience and reach more people with the right message at the right time. Can you only do that with Ads? Heck, no! You can do that with other audience growing strategies too!

I teach a combination of ways to achieve Audience growth, which is the A within the L.E.A.P Method™.

One of these is the Partnership Plan™ which you use to leverage other people's audiences to connect with relevant future clients and to grow your own audience. It is a combination of strategies that get you in front of other people's audiences in a credible way. When done correctly, you attract new clients into your funnel and your coaching offers. The best thing is, the Partnership Plan™ audience-growth strategies are completely free.

Don't get me wrong, Ads are great if you have the budget and want to speed the process up, but they're not necessary.

If you hold on to the belief that you don't want to use evergreen marketing because it requires you to use Ads, you will miss out on being able to sign new clients every month. Or you can choose to go evergreen and utilise all the free audience-growth strategies at your fingertips.

PART 5

PROFIT

13

A PROFIT MOTIVE

TWO DAYS before my thirtieth birthday I sat next to Sir Richard Branson on Necker Island drinking strawberry daiquiris, and I asked him a question:

"You've built successful businesses, you've led teams, you've achieved incredible things, and you've had to make millions of decisions to get you here. So what are the core ingredients of good decisions and what have been some of your best decisions?"

I'll share his answer with you in a moment, but first I'll tell you the story behind the reason I asked him this question. I could have asked him any question, so why this one?

Imagine you're with us at dinner that night, over forty self-made women millionaires, or very soon to be millionaires, who made their millions through having their own business; what do you immediately assume about these people?

You might assume they are the hardest workers you've ever met. Or you might fathom that they are the most educated people. Or maybe they are all in sales because you believe that being in sales is the most direct way to make money. Maybe you assume they're simply lucky. Or maybe you think they frugally saved and invested their money to create their millions.

These are all fair assumptions to make. But they're only fair because that's what you've been led to believe by today's societal norms. These assumptions have been keeping you stuck where you are. In fact, I'd go as far as to say that these assumptions keep you over-worked, under-paid and without the freedom you were placed on this planet to enjoy.

As an entrepreneur, one of the reasons you started your business was probably because you saw it as a way of blowing the ceiling off your earning potential while doing work you love and setting your own schedule.

You'd been boxed into a corporate role that wasn't using your strengths. It required you to be someone you're not just to succeed. Or maybe you'd gone through the traditional schooling system and felt like you never truly fit because it wasn't designed for out-of-the-box thinkers like you. Somewhere along your path, you ended up with a deep inner knowing that you were meant for something bigger. You knew that entrepreneurship was going to allow you to tap into that, so you could create more financial success and personal happiness than ever before.

But let me ask you, are you really making more money by running your current business versus being employed? I'm talking about the money you personally take home and not your business's topline revenue.

If you're like most entrepreneurs, when you calculate your average hourly rate based on the money you took home last month and the number of hours you worked in the business, you might be financially better off getting a job at your local cute coffee shop and trading it in for a more stress-free life. But that's not what you want for yourself. You want the freedom to set your own schedule, to create what you want to create rather than what your boss needs from you and to know that there's no glass ceiling to what you can achieve and earn.

What you didn't expect about being an entrepreneur, though, was just how hard you would need to work and how often there isn't enough money in the bank to pay yourself the amount you deserve given how much time, effort and risk you've taken on for your business. What has led you to be overworked and underpaid is not your fault. At least, not entirely.

But unless something drastic changes, you risk continuing to work hard in your business without ever really experiencing an increase in your personal wealth. If you've been pedalling along in your business for quite some time, making personal sacrifices like missing social events, working weekends and skipping exercise you know your body needs... if your relationships or health have suffered and you've found yourself in some financial hot water along the way, you know something has to change in the way you do things if you want to hold on to your sanity, partner and health.

Ditch Your Industrial-Age Thinking

The hidden system you've been working within is rigged against you right now. It's time to stop working like an industrial-age worker.

The Industrial Revolution of the eighteenth century was based on factory production as the source of wealth creation. It led to humans working between twelve and fourteen hours a day, six days a week because the factory owners didn't want to turn off the machines that were producing output. Productivity, then, was equal to how long workers worked at the assembly lines.

As an industrial-age worker, the hours you worked and the production you created directed the income you made. This way of working has been passed down through the generations to you and me today.

You might have grandparents who worked themselves to the bone in a mine, in a factory or on a farm like mine did, because that was the main way in which most of our ancestors created income back then. Not only was this way of working passed down to you, the beliefs that come along with it were also passed down. "You must work hard to make money" and "no pain, no gain" reinforce the idea in your head that to create financial success, you must personally sacrifice a great deal.

Today, you have other opportunities. You have so many ways of making money with more technology, information and connectivity than ever before. This means that instead of working hard in a way that feels overly self-sacrificing, you have the opportunity to work in a way that leverages technology and allows you to achieve so much more with far less effort.

Continuing to operate in your business from the old paradigm that you must work your way to wealth – and that your time spent working is the direct indicator of the amount of money you make – will only ever leave you burnt out, underpaid and overworked.

It's time to stop working like an industrial-age worker.

Do you need to be frugal to thrive financially?

Books like *The Millionaire Next Door* by Thomas J. Stanley and William D. Danko share how you can become a self-made millionaire through reducing your personal expenses and squirrelling money away every month over a long period of time. Of course, with the benefit of compound interest you become an eventual millionaire.

However, if you don't enjoy the idea of sacrificing your day-to-day spending and always going for the cheapest option when you desire something else, then I understand that. It's never really appealed to me either.

I don't think I've ever created a budget that I've stuck to, even though I've tried a couple of times. Something in my heart tells me that I'm not meant to live in restriction or a state of lack. I take a stand for the "and" and choose to live in a state of expansiveness. This means that you can live a comfortable life *and* invest money into your long-term wealth; it doesn't have to be an either/or, because your financial success and the money you make, I believe, can expand with your level of desire.

If you've ever found yourself in a situation where you have tried to keep to a budget but you never manage to stick to it, you'll know that sacrificial saving probably won't be your path to wealth.

Take a stand for the 'and' and choose to live in a state of expansiveness. If you're looking for a way of making millions that does not require you to buy the cheapest of everything available, I want to offer you an alternative.

Do Good Grades Equal Good Money?

If you were brought up in the traditional schooling systems that exist across the world, you have probably been conditioned to believe that it's typically the most educated people with the best grades who make the most money; that for you to succeed in life financially, you must finish school and get good exam results so you can land a high-paying job. If you decide to bomb out of school or you're just not great at exams, your lifetime earning potential will suffer. Whether you were consciously aware of this societal conditioning being imprinted on you or not, most people are led to think this way.

However, if being wealthy was based on how educated you are, every highly educated person would be abundantly well off, and we know that isn't the case. You might even know some people who aren't well educated at all yet have thriving businesses and finances. My father is a classic example of this. He's so dyslexic that I often can't understand his text messages. He hated school, yet he and my mother have gone on to create thriving businesses together.

He didn't rely on education to get him there; he used something else.

Make Good Decisions to Avoid Burnout

As a mentor to hundreds of female entrepreneurs over the last few years, I often work with very high-achieving women who have created impressive success in their current business, a previous business or their former corporate life. But as high achievers, they have typically found themselves in a state of major burnout. As they build their current business, many of them share their worry about not wanting to find themselves in a state of burnout again because they've worked too hard.

Their fear of needing to burn their business to the ground or take a long period of time off to recover is very real. They know that overworking comes at the cost of their physical and mental health, as well as potentially placing them in a tricky financial situation when they can no longer sustain a high level of output.

When you have experienced a low point like major burnout, you'll do everything in your power to avoid it happening again, including choosing to not grow your business, to take smaller risks and to play small for fear of your health suffering.

Here's how that thinking is faulty and leads you to only ever operate at below fifty percent of your potential. Your burnout was driven by the decisions you made along the way – both consciously and unconsciously. This means you have the power to pivot your own direction and avoid a repeat of your past burnout by choosing to make different decisions. You have the personal power to make different decisions that lead you to an entirely different outcome.

If you're a recovered burnt out high achiever, look back at the months and years that led to your burnout. Did you say yes to work that wasn't aligned with your core strengths or values? Were you working in a way that only ever depleted you? Did your inner people pleaser stop you saying no when you wanted to? Did you over-work because you felt on some level that you weren't good enough and needed to overcompensate?

When you realise that all you need to do is get really good at making the right decisions for yourself to create wild financial success in your business without the burnout, your fear can melt away and be replaced by a deep sense of personal power.

Deciding Your Way to Wealth

Your best ideas can come from your darkest moments. In March 2021, I stared at the ceiling, exhausted, from my bedroom floor.

I was running a business that was making £20,000 (about $25,000) in cash every month, but we were only just breaking even after I'd paid my team, expenses, tax and a "just enough" salary to myself to cover my mortgage and living expenses. It had been like this for well over eight months. I really wanted to grow the business. I really wanted to create more profit so the business could begin to pay me more and allow me to invest in other wealth-generating assets.

I could see other people leading businesses in my industry that were generating six figures in cash every month, so why couldn't I? Why was I so darn stuck?

If I wanted to double the business income every month, I would need to double how long and hard I was working. But I was already at full capacity, so there was no way that was possible.

That was the point at which I realised the assumption I was making about what it takes to create financial success in my business was completely wrong. In that moment, the penny dropped and I finally saw the unconscious and hugely restrictive belief I'd been operating from that had led me here: You have to work hard to make money.

I was clearly the product of societal conditioning that had led me to believe that the wealth we generate is down to our output: how hard and long we work. But what if that were wrong? What if there were an alternative way to generate wealth – financial wealth and all the other forms of wealth: joy, love, health, personal freedom and so much more?

What if, instead of working my way to wealth, what if… I could *decide* my way to wealth? What if it was no longer about how hard I was willing to work, and instead down to how good I was at making the right decisions? Could I catapult my financial success in an instant by making the right choice versus the wrong choice?

As I got off the floor, I made a commitment to myself: to master the art of deciding my way to wealth.

What happened next? I rapidly scaled the business from £20,000 cash months to double that in five months. Eleven months later, I'd quadrupled the monthly cash flow and only added an extra fifty percent in monthly expenses. That's £30,000 in monthly operating costs and £80,000 in cash received, just to really spell it out.

On top of that, I experienced my most joyful year to date and had started working fewer than thirty hours a week. To be clear, the joy didn't come from the money, although it did allow me to buy things I really value. It came from the powerful decisions I made.

Of all the other ways to create wealth – being highly educated, working the hardest or saving your way there – I find the ability to decide your way to wealth is by far the most exciting way to lead your business and life. It's simple. And it's the ultimate ladder in the game of Snakes and Ladders.

The reality you have today is for the most part a result of the compounded decisions you've made to date. This means your reality tomorrow and in the years to come can be shaped by you so that you end up where you actually want to be in your business and life, rather than look back and wonder how the heck things went so sideways.

Learning to decide your way to wealth allows you to feel deeply powerful in any situation, because you know you have the ability to shift course at any given moment in your business.

Why don't you make your first conscious wealth-building decision right now?

Barbara Huson is a financial therapist to women and author of numerous books, including *Secrets of Six Figure Women*; based on extensive research and hundreds of interviews, including more than one hundred and fifty women whose annual earnings ranged from $100,000 to $7 million, Huson discovered there were seven core strategies for upping earnings.

The first is to have a 'Profit Motive'; high-earning women expect to be compensated well for their work and feel good rather than guilty about earning money.

If you've been needing permission to make as much money as you want to, this is it. Today is the day you get to choose to have an Unapologetic Profit Motive.

Sir Richard Branson answered my question on Necker Island by sharing a framework of thinking. He said that many entrepreneurs start out by trying to "save the world" in some way, without first "saving" and looking after themselves financially, let alone their family and local community. When those entrepreneurs struggle to get their impact-driven business off the ground fast enough to look after themselves and their families from the profit they generate, they have to give up the dream too soon.

In the same way that you're taught to put your own mask on before helping others in an emergency on a plane, Branson shared that we all operate within four concentric circles of support: you supporting you, you supporting your family, then your local community, and then your country or the world. We must start at the innermost circle and work our way outwards.

That doesn't mean you shouldn't give to charity once you're personally financially free. Nor is this about being selfish. It's about pouring into your own cup so you can pour into others' cups with far more gusto in the future. Of course, for you to be financially successful in a business, you have to help a lot of people by selling them something that's truly going to serve them. But don't let helping a lot of people come at the cost of yourself. There is no place for feeling guilty or selfish about having a clear profit motive and more than enough money when you're growing your income by helping more people.

It's Not About the Money

I love money. I love money because of what you can do with it. Money itself is cool, but it's mainly just a bunch of numbers on a screen and it's not the best at deep conversations about love, the universe and the meaning of life.

However, having a lot of money means you can do, experience and have a lot of things in your life that matter to you. Even though money itself can't necessarily make you happy, if you know how to spend or invest $10 in a way that brings you joy, you'll know how to manage $1,000,000 in a way that makes you happy too.

Having a profit motive becomes a whole more exciting when you know what meaningful purpose the profit has in your life and your family's life. So here comes the exciting question: what do you want to do with all the profit you generate? What would light you up?

14

YOUR MILLIONAIRE PERMISSION SLIP

Investment, Break Even and Profit Phases

LOOKING BACK at my own journey, from raiding my entire personal savings to the growing business I have today, I realise that there are three major phases to building a successful business. Many entrepreneurs give up during phase one because they don't understand the entire journey.

In the first phase (Investment) you put more effort, time and money into your business than you get back. The payoff doesn't match your personal sacrifice in the moment. This phase can last a short or long time and is usually shortened by knowing where to spend your time and money to get the best results (which can be helped by having good mentors), by reaching a good product-market fit faster, and by lowering your expectations of results so you don't talk yourself into giving up too soon.

I spent two years in this phase and it felt like I was giving myself an entire online MBA through all the education I invested time in and the trial and error I went through. Thankfully, one of my mentors happened to mention that she found it often takes two years for an online coaching business to really build momentum from scratch. I didn't have an expectation of overnight success.

Eventually, you reach the break even phase, where the money you receive is equal to the effort you put in. This phase is really exciting because it gives you so much hope of what's to come, but it can lead to some useless purchases spent on things that don't lead to growth in your business. Instead of massively upgrading your lifestyle and increasing your personal expenses because you feel you've "earned" it, this is where great financial management will save you from ballooning and then rapidly contracting again.

It is critical at this point to master the art of deciding your way to wealth. Reinvest these profits into systems, people and assets that will pay off in the future. This is the only pathway to reaching phase three where a huge payoff is available to you.

I spent about another two years in phase two before entering phase three and reaching a life-changing net profit margin of fifty percent and more.

Initially, I feared sharing the volume of profit the business was consistently generating per month. But then looking back at this journey, I realised I'd spent years "buying" and truly earning the profit I was experiencing, which helped evaporate fears of judgement from others or guilt of now "having it easy". I knew those who truly understood the phases of the entrepreneurial journey would not take issue with or judge the phase we had reached.

Phase three is created by the growth compound of great decision-making. These decisions are focused on investing money and time into your team, systems, audience growth, your skillset as a CEO, great client delivery and creating business assets. If you quit too early in phase one or don't make great decisions in phase two, you will find yourself starting over.

Even though it's not sexy compared to the short-term massive wins that a big launch or seemingly overnight success may appear to be, playing for the long-term and being patient will mean you take multiple thousands and maybe even millions of dollars in profit home personally in the end.

Your Big Ass Permission Slip

Your business is an investment similar to investing in property or the stock market. You essentially have shares in your own company. But you're also investing your energy and your time, which you probably don't do anywhere near as much with property or stock market investments. So I want to give you permission to make a shit tonne of money in your business, because it needs to give you more money than your property and stock market investments if you give it all this extra time and energy.

I believe one of the reasons that only two percent of female entrepreneurs generate a million dollars in revenue is because they don't give themselves permission to make a tonne of money from their business. But why is it socially acceptable for us to make millions from property or the stock market? Why does that feel different?

For you to create a million dollars in your coaching business, you have to deliver at least a million dollars of value to others, and often far more. That value will impact people's lives in some way, whether you coach and teach in the realms of marketing and sales, health and wellness, or love and relationships.

Is that type of value more valuable to the greater collective than an increase in the value of a property or the stock market? Quite possibly. I want to give you a Big Ass Permission Slip to go and impact all the people and make all the money you want.

Women focus on impact too quickly, rather than wealth, because we want to be liked so much.

Here's the frustrating truth, based on research. We know that women who have perceived power are also perceived to be less likeable, by both men and women, compared to an equivalent man with an equivalent level of power.

Let's be honest, money equals power, so more money means more power in many ways. We often find ourselves as women bending our own boundaries for others to like us, rather than saying yes or no to the things that will lead us to generate more financial success. Have you ever lowered your prices for a friend, for instance?

Instead of spending time overstepping your own boundaries to please others, I invite you to spend more time really moving the needle on the things that matter to you most based on your definition of wealth, whether financially or holistically. Let's be honest, there's no award given to people who get to the end of their career and aren't able to support themselves financially in retirement. Does finding yourself in that situation make you more or less likeable? That's kind of a silly question, right?

In a world where women often focus on impact too quickly rather than wealth, because we want to be liked so much, I want to show you how you can truly have both for yourself: meaningful impact *and* personal wealth. Serving clients through a valuable group coaching program that sells year-round on evergreen, without the need for exhausting launches, is one of the most empowering, fun and freedom-orientated ways to do exactly that.

Your mother couldn't do what we can do now in the online industry, because she didn't get the chance. The internet wasn't around and the coaching industry was still in its infancy. Your ability to create the life you want, to help a lot of people across the world with your expertise and to transform your personal finances as a result of your business has changed in one generation.

I'm insanely grateful to be living on this planet at this time and I hope you are too. There has never been a better time in history to launch, run and grow a wildly successful business that genuinely transforms other people's lives across the world. Your time is NOW. You'd be bonkers to miss the opportunity.

PART 6

NEXT STEPS

15

COMMON ROADBLOCKS TO EVERGREEN SUCCESS

BEFORE YOU VENTURE into building your own profitable and scalable evergreen business, I want to give you a heads-up on some of the challenges you may come across that have the potential to throttle your success.

Having helped countless entrepreneurs build successful evergreen funnels and programs, I've noticed four common barriers that hold them back from generating the results they're capable of.

1. Your messaging isn't sharp enough

You can build a kickass evergreen webinar funnel and implement every single step involved, but if your messaging is vague and you're speaking to two or three different ideal clients throughout the funnel, your overall conversion rate will suffer.

Many coaches stop themselves from getting specific enough with their messaging and it prevents their businesses from truly taking off. They fear excluding some people who could be potential clients by being too specific and worry they'll miss out on potential sales. Some feel resistant to hanging their hat on one core message because they're multi-passionate entrepreneurs and don't want to box themselves in. If this is one of your top concerns too, I want you to know that committing to a really specific message in your funnel is not the same as committing to a really specific message for your entire business.

You will probably have one good funnel that leads to your core program, a down-sell for those who aren't ready for your main offer yet, and an upsell offer for those who graduate from your core program.

However, if you have more than one core offer, you will probably have another funnel leading to your next offer. This does add more complexity to your business because you're almost running two businesses at this point, but it is possible. I did this for half of 2022. I wouldn't advise it before you hit seven figures as it adds a lot of unnecessary work and it's often far easier and more profitable to scale what you already have.

Some entrepreneurs hold back from being specific enough because they worry they'll annoy the people who might disagree with their messaging. Their innate desire to be liked by others stops them from standing out from the crowd by taking a stand for what they believe in.

In the first few weeks of going all in on my messaging about ditching the launch roller coaster reliance and going evergreen instead, I got a lot of unfollows on Instagram and I heard that I was being spoken about behind my back in other circles. The thing that kept me going was knowing that my specific ideal client, who didn't enjoy launching or didn't want to do it at all, was in need of my solution.

I know my programs are not for everyone and neither is yours. Your messaging may not resonate with those it's not meant for, and it may cause others who sit on the other side of the fence to disagree with you.

This is fine. You are safe for others to disagree with you. You are safe for others to not like you all the time. You are safe to take a stand for your ideal person who needs to hear about your specific solution, and who truly needs you to show up for them so their problem can be solved with your support.

Some entrepreneurs hold themselves back from being specific enough in their messaging simply because they haven't taken the time to get to know their ideal client inside out yet. Research interviews, DM conversations and interviews with your favourite clients will quickly close this gap for you.

When you nail your messaging for your funnel, you can see the results from a mile off and you can lace that same messaging through all your other marketing channels: your podcast, social media content, YouTube channel and guest trainings. This means you're consistent across all channels and your audience will trust you even more.

Don't let the fear that your messaging isn't sharp enough yet stop you from making the shift to go evergreen. The process of going evergreen is itself the perfect opportunity to test, refine and get fast feedback on what resonates and what doesn't. Trying to work out your messaging in your head without much testing will leave you stuck in the same place months later. Going evergreen has been the birth process for so many of my client's sharp messaging.

2. You secretly believe evergreen isn't going to work for you

Has someone told you that you need to have a bigger online community before you can successfully go evergreen? Or maybe you paid a marketing agency to set up the funnels and Ads for you but it didn't work out, and if the experts can't do it then how are you meant to? Or maybe you're so used to launching that you're in a state of "I'll believe it when I see it" when it comes to creating sales outside of a launch. Somewhere along the way, you stop the results from happening; you lose interest, don't give it enough of a chance to truly take off and decide it simply doesn't work for you and your offer.

All strategies work on some level, it's simply a case of deciding how you want to do business. If you're sold on the idea of clients signing up to work with you every week with ease, don't give up on that dream so fast. It absolutely can and will work for you.

3. You give up too soon

I am often asked how quickly you can create results when you first go evergreen with your group coaching program. The answer really varies depending on many factors.

I've seen clients create a $40,000 month in the first thirty days, others who have turned their program evergreen within two weeks of us beginning to work together, and I've also seen clients take three to six months to get the ball rolling because they changed their mind about what they wanted to sell, or they frankly didn't have a reason to do things quickly because income to support them was coming in from other sources.

One thing I know to be true is that going evergreen is one of the best compounding games you can play in your business. In my first attempt at going evergreen, I signed nine clients in nine weeks just by spending $30 a day on Ads.

After going backwards and forwards between that strategy and launching for more than twelve months, I re-committed to going all in on the evergreen approach and in month one, I signed just one client. It took an entire three weeks for that first client to sign up, and to be honest, I'm pretty sure she was a referral and didn't even go through my funnel.

In the second month, I signed three clients but not until the second half of the month, so there were a number of weeks where the tumbleweed was blowing, but I kept the faith because I believed in what I was sharing and knew that my online community simply needed to catch up on the new messaging and offer I was marketing.

In month three, I signed five clients in the first two weeks of the month, and that was mostly down to going all in on finding five amazing humans to work with. The "all in" energy helped a lot. In the following month, I brought in an insane eleven clients into the Freedom Accelerator.

The strategy had compounded enough and we turned a corner. I'd changed nothing about my funnel in the weeks preceding this.

We then dialled it down a little and I've consistently signed four to six clients a month ever since. Some months will be slower but I don't worry about it because I know what levers to pull to bring in more results, and I know there are bigger months coming when I want to create them.

Was it worth waiting four months to get to this point? Absolutely! Would it have been worth waiting even longer, even six or eight months, to have created the same result? Definitely!

If you're used to big cash injections from launches and you have a habit of upgrading your expenses and lifestyle every time you do a launch, I recommend being cautious as you shift into evergreen. Either lean out your expenses a little to remove any worry about running out of money in the transition, or simply create income from elsewhere such as one-to-one clients or ad-hoc consulting so you have the spaciousness to ramp up your evergreen sales without the pressure of it needing to work right away, just in case.

I've seen clients generate far faster results than this, which is always great to see. It's also part of the coaching journey: you're coaching your clients to be better than you. Even though you may find that triggering, it's one of the best compliments you can get as a coach, so I love it when my clients beat my records.

4. You cap out on your delivery capacity

Once you hit a certain number of people in your group program, it's easy to get stuck and not be able to sign any more clients above that number because you feel like you've hit your maximum capacity for what you can hold. The number differs for everyone, but you'll intuitively know when you hit it.

You might decide that the ceiling you hit in your client delivery capacity is just right for you and you're not too worried about making your container any larger. In other cases, you know you could be helping so many more people and you want to blow your own ceiling off.

If you're in the latter situation, here are the top reasons why coaches hold themselves back from growing:

#1 You're treating each client like a one-to-one client with direct message access to you or additional random one-to-one calls, without that being agreed upfront. You're spending a tonne of time in client delivery mode, while also creating a co-dependent relationship with them, rather than empowering them.

#2 You're taking full responsibility for client results and then semi-freaking out if a client doesn't get them. Instead of seeing your clients as deeply powerful beings in their own right, you feel you must plug every gap for them, including doing the work for them to get results.

#3 You let one not-so-great client in the group stop you from marketing and selling more places into the group. That one individual negatively impacts the dynamic of the group so much that you don't feel comfortable signing your absolute dream clients up into the same container, for fear of what they might think.

#4 You're responding to all client questions within a few hours (sometimes within minutes) and creating a co-dependent client-coach relationship, which also means you rarely get a chance to focus on the tasks you have at hand when it comes to running your business.

#5 You're trying to meet everyone's needs with zero guard rails, so in any given call you're solving problems on topics as varied as money mindset, marriage challenges, messaging clarity and managing taxes because you've become the go-to for everything, rather than setting expectations for how to make the most out of group coaching calls. This leaves you feeling stretched and in some way not as great at your job as you want to be, because you're not playing in your true zone of genius on the calls.

#6 You didn't design your group coaching container and its client result systems with scale in mind in the first place. When you're scaling your delivery capacity with client results in mind, there are a few things you need to get right, including having a clear pathway and checkpoints for monitoring client progress.

Even if you have your group program running right now, you can make changes to it mid-flight. I've upgraded the delivery model multiple times over the three years of running my core group program.

#7 You're not willing to let go of some parts of your client delivery. Hiring other experts and coaches to take on a part of your client delivery role can be incredibly hard when you care so much about the delivery quality. But when you're able to find the right person and take the leap to hand over some client delivery responsibilities, you open up a whole new world of potential for serving more clients.

Hopefully, this list has helped you identify where your biggest opportunities are for expanding your capacity to help more people and ultimately bust through your own self-imposed income ceiling.

16

WHERE FROM HERE?

WE'VE COVERED a lot of ground together throughout this book. I hope you see just how life-changing having a group coaching program on evergreen can be for both you and your clients.

But what else do you need to be successful? A few more pieces of the puzzle are required to create success and it simply isn't possible to provide them through a book alone; namely, individual feedback and personalisation, accountability, community and context. These factors all rapidly shorten your timeline for creating results.

Receiving individual feedback and personalising the frameworks for evergreen success to your own situation is a total game changer. Applying a generic evergreen strategy into your business without adaptation is a recipe for frustration and potential failure.

For example, you've probably taken a course before and learned some cool new things, but then struggled to implement what you've learned in a way that feels good to you and creates results in your unique situation. This is where being part of a group coaching program that has personalisation and feedback built in leads you to create far greater results than by figuring it out alone.

For example, one of the keys to evergreen success is your ability to craft and clearly articulate the value of your offer. Refining your messaging and sharpening your ability to communicate the value of your program is critical to being able to make sales every week. Many people tie themselves in knots with this piece and would benefit hugely from receiving feedback on their messaging, copy and how they articulate their value.

Information is available for free and very cheaply. Personalised support for implementation and receiving feedback from experts is the difference between mediocre results and life-changing growth in your business. In other words, you often don't need more content to learn; you need more guidance within your unique context.

Another part of truly scaling your business is about your ability to lead, both your team and your clients. You need to handle difficult situations, from firing people to client complaints, and from legal stress to scaling client delivery with client results in mind.

These difficult situations may put you right off growing your business but I've learnt that even if dealing with these difficult situations is the worst part of my job, the juice is still absolutely worth the squeeze and I really don't mind having to find solutions to these kinds of problems.

Don't get me wrong, I don't welcome them in! But when there's a problem, your job as CEO is to respond with presence, personal power and processes. The reason I can say that is that I've had great mentors and consulting support along the way as my business has grown, so I've been able to learn from their experience and expertise when I've not known what to do.

I love being able to guide my clients in these situations too. Otherwise, without proper guidance, you can easily and quickly downward spiral yourself into wanting to chuck the entire business into the trash and walk away when you're not confident in how to deal with difficult situations. Another gap you will need to have solutions for to be able to leverage what I've shared with you in this book is your marketing aptitude.

Without understanding how to take leads down the buyer decision-making process in your funnel and convert content into clients (both of which I have a proven, adaptable framework to help you in), as well as understanding how to effectively retarget the people who have come into your world so your conversion rate can go up, you'll always miss out on potential clients.

Similarly, without a clear step-by-step process for going evergreen that is specifically laid out in the fastest, most effective way, including templates and examples to speed you up, and without knowing what data to look out for on your funnel and what iterations to make to increase profit, there's little use in having an evergreen funnel. It's like wanting a slice of your favourite homemade chocolate cake but only having the ingredients for a Victoria sponge. It isn't going to satisfy the chocolate craving, no matter how much Victoria sponge you eat! Anyone can create an evergreen funnel but not everyone knows how to accurately use it as a tool for rapid business growth.

The last element is personal accountability, your mindset and the degree to which you let the Mindset Monkeys rule your head and therefore your results.

Leading a group of over fifty women when you're often the youngest in the room, as is often the case at my current age, is one hell of a leadership growth opportunity. Being able to handle various preferences, personalities and rates of progress within clients is not for the faint of heart. But I've learned to adore the personal growth that leading a group of powerful women has given me.

If entrepreneurship is just one big personal development journey with a dollop of money-making thrown in (if you do it right), then leading a group of incredible clients is that same personal development journey but on steroids.

This is one of the most important reasons for having a mentor who's gone before you and has handled all the challenging situations before so can guide you.

Being in a community of other people who are on the same path and dealing with the same challenges as you is priceless as you grow your business. You always have a listening ear, a tactical piece of input or simply a safe space to share. All ships rise with the tide together, so if you want to rapidly expand your success, get yourself into communities where creating wild success is normal.

When you're among people on a similar path, you soon learn that client feedback that feels like a complaint, a refund request, a client in victimhood, a lead that's ghosted you and all the other triggering and hard situations you come across are perfectly normal. Thankfully, you can do hard things. Whatever shit storm is thrown at you will pass, and you'll come out stronger on the other side, because you have that powerful community around you.

One of my team members asked me an interesting question recently: "When it comes to your ideal clients and community, what about their struggles breaks your heart?"

I responded with a rather heated voice note and I honestly got a little angry about this one. Not because I was mad about the question. When I talk about this, it always gets me going. It's when I see women who have so much value in them – whether that's expertise or experience – and there's so much they could help others with, yet they aren't making the money that they so clearly could and deserve to make in their business. It is mainly because they haven't been able to figure out how to make the business work for them, and they're not signing the clients they want or charging the prices they want to.

They haven't yet cracked the code to sharing their value in a way that means they are massively compensated for it. It makes me so angry that these women don't end up creating the financial resources that they so clearly deserve, because I see it so blindingly clearly for them. I see the blocks keeping them from wild success, and I see precisely what's on the other side of those blocks for them.

Freedom, purpose, simplicity.

From booking a luxe Airbnb without looking at the rates, or hiring someone to cook healthy meals at home, or retiring their partner. It's all available! It's right there!

That's what I want for you too. I wrote this book to show you that it's entirely possible for you to create the lifestyle and time freedom you crave, the financial abundance you deserve and to help a lot of people in a way that lights you up.

I hope you feel inspired and brimming with motivation to get started on growing your own group coaching program on evergreen, so you can transform more lives with your work, build a stable income in your business and have the space to enjoy your life without being a slave to your business.

So what's the best way to get started on doing exactly that?

You're invited to apply to join us in our industry-leading Freedom Accelerator program. The application process is quick and easy, and there's nothing to lose by enquiring to see if this is the right fit for you.

Head to go.roseradford.com/apply and you'll receive a response from me and the team within a few days.

If you're not getting the results you want in your business right now, you have a blind spot or two holding you back from breaking through to your next level of success. By definition, you cannot see your own blind spots. By filling that gap with things you didn't know you don't know right now, the women I work with radically transform their results in a short period of time. Often, just the smallest of tweaks make the biggest of differences.

This is not because you're not capable. You're more than capable of reaching your goals and achieving the vision you have for your business and life, and you may want to avoid the trial and error of figuring it out yourself and speed up the process.

If you're ready for a breakthrough, I'd love to receive your application.

17

FAQS AND MINDSET FUNKS STANDING IN YOUR WAY

THIS CHAPTER IS PROBABLY the most valuable encore to a book ever, even though I say so myself. I have a feeling you will love this collection of frequently asked questions and common mindset barriers that stand in the way of your success.

Question: Sh*t, I can see how this is going to totally work and now I'm scared of my own success.

I used to believe that running a business generating a million dollars a year in revenue would come with so many downsides that I wouldn't want to do it. In fact, I believed that turning over $1,000,000 a year would be harder work than making $200,000 a year.

I was wrong. I have found it far easier because once I reached the million-dollar mark, I knew what I was selling and how to sell it, and I had cash to pay my team so I was doing less of the operational work.

I also used to believe that running and paying for a team would feel like a burden. Again, not true. When your team are income-generating or know how to truly add value to the business, this feels like less of an issue. Also, monthly recurring revenue and building a cash reserve removes the fear about paying your team every month.

The responsibility of supporting the number of clients required to create a million in revenue felt far too overwhelming when I was making just ten percent of that income per year. Again, this wasn't true. I realised that I'm not actually responsible for my clients, and I'd never want to be anyway because they're deeply powerful humans in their own right. I am, however, responsible for delivering on the promise and contract I have with them.

Can you see the pattern here? Our assumptions and fears about success are often well off the mark.

I discovered that creating a bigger business and more outward success led me to be able to do, have and experience things I would never have been able to otherwise. Creating wild success allowed me to relocate my husband and myself to our dream country. It allowed me to run two transformational client retreats, travel to Necker Island, have a beautiful wedding without worrying about the budget, and rent a gorgeous apartment in central Lisbon that had enough room for lots of friends to stay comfortably.

All of these things gave me so much joy. I realised that when success is created in alignment with your innate self-expression – rather than from ego – there's no need to worry about the potential downsides.

Question: I want to do this but I'm really scared (of failing, of the unknown, of lions...). What's your advice?

> "A good life is the culmination of curiosity and being in the race."
>
> SIR RICHARD BRANSON

We create ourselves by the actions we take.

Small goals lead to small actions. Big goals lead to big actions. I've almost always set big goals and then got between seventy and ninety percent of the way there, or I've got there but it just took longer than I expected.

If your goals aren't big enough, you're probably already aware of that and don't need me to tell you. Instead of harping on about how you need to have big goals to decide your way to wealth, I'd rather talk to you about the courage you will need to propel yourself forwards once you've set a big goal. Anyone can set a big goal, but not everyone can achieve that big goal. That latter requires courage.

I made one of the most courageous and defining decisions of my life while lying on my bed staring at the ceiling.

I'd been trying to get my business off the ground for at least a year but was going around in circles trying to clarify what I was selling and to whom. I kept losing faith in myself and having a "crisis of clarity" for a few weeks until I thought I'd found "my thing", only to find myself back in a crisis of clarity, self-doubt, overthinking and fear again just a few weeks later.

I was desperate to get my business off the ground, to begin to actually sell something and create momentum. I saw other people doing what I wanted to do, so I knew it was possible for me too, but perfectionism and self-doubt kept taking over and holding me back.

I flopped onto my bed in another crisis of clarity and stared up at the bedroom ceiling feeling immensely frustrated with myself. Then I made the most ridiculous decision.

Despite having absolutely zero evidence suggesting it was true, I decided to play at the top of my industry. I simply decided I was already at the top of my industry and I began to act, think and decide in alignment with that chosen reality for myself. I could have easily told myself that I was a joke for thinking of such a ridiculous idea, given I didn't have the success, brand, money or clients to show for it.

To be clear, I never lied about the success I had created, or rather, had not created (yet!). I simply began to show up as the version of me who had already created wild success. That looked like getting more visible online, taking courageous action whenever I saw the opportunity, hosting live events in London and throwing my hat into the ring for opportunities I would normally have decided I wasn't good enough for yet.

This decision to play at the top required radical belief in the unseen. It required me to stop relying on certainty, something that is only ever based on physical evidence. Instead, it required me to rely on courage.

When you do not have evidence of your ability, you cannot have certainty in your ability. If you only ever relied on certainty as an entrepreneur, you would end up staying in the same place forever. Where there is no certainty, you must rely on courage.

Certainty and courage are equally as valuable and reliable. Your courage and radical belief in the unseen in the pursuit of your business goals can sometimes feel like you're a little crazy, or as if you're kidding yourself. But it is that leap of courage that will separate you from the limited, fearful version of you and will catapult you into wild, unparalleled success. Don't all the geniuses look a little crazy from the outside?

One of my clients once asked me how she can find more comfort in being able to sell her new offer even though she's not certain about the result it creates just yet, because the evidence of the clients creating results isn't there yet, given she's only just launched the offer.

This was a classic situation in which courage must take the lead over certainty. In a chicken and egg situation like this, where you can't sell your new offer before having certainty in your offer and you can't have certainty in your offer until you've had clients create results from it, but you can't have that happen until you've sold it... you must break the cycle and the best circuit breaker is courage.

I think about people like Elon Musk, who has a vision for humans living on Mars, despite there still being major barriers to that, which our latest scientific findings don't have solutions for right now. Yet his courageous conviction in his vision is enough to garner large amounts of money to support the creation of it, and to attract leading scientists to pursue answers to the remaining problems.

Elon's vision may be too "out there" for you to relate to, but I bet you can think of at least one person you know who acts with courage and believes in their inevitable success no matter what.

Question: Do I need to hire a marketing team to be able to go evergreen?

Hiring a marketing team or an ads manager to do this for you and handing responsibility over is a really easy trap to fall into. The CEO Coach, on the other hand, empowers herself with the knowledge she needs to make money.

She discovers that a good team that will get her results costs between $3,000 and $4,000 a month or more. So rather than handing this responsibility over to somebody whose biggest interest is in running their own agency rather than driving revenue in your business, empower yourself with the skill sets first and save yourself a lot of money in the process.

In the first few years of running my business, I used to judge myself for becoming a "marketer" to grow my business. My inner snob thought it was below me. Goodness knows where I got that idea from.

I saw myself as an entrepreneur, not a – dare I say it – lowly marketer. Somewhere along the way, I'd come to believe that being a marketer has a stigma attached to it that I didn't want to adopt for myself. I wish I could tell that twenty-six-year-old Rose to get over her damn self and do the darn thing.

I now love having, using and teaching a marketing skill set. The thing that really blows my mind is that I have Marketing and Sales Coaches as clients, and they're learning marketing and sales from me – go figure!

I was asked what I did for a living at a friend's wedding recently and once I explained, my newly acquired friend asked me what training I'd done in marketing and sales. I paused for a moment and replied, "I suppose I'm completely self-taught. I dodged all the marketing and sales modules in my business degree because I didn't think they'd be useful to me."

I say this so you know it's entirely possible for you to learn these skills from scratch too. And it's critical that you do, because you can have the best product or service in the world but if nobody knows about it then it doesn't matter. Giving yourself the sales and marketing skill set is one of the best gifts you could ever give yourself.

Question: I feel I've been burned by previous experiences of investing in business coaching so I feel gun-shy about investing again to grow my business. What words of advice would you give to me?

Even though it was a cold November day, I was hot and sweaty from running across London Heathrow Airport. When

I got to the gate our plane to Chile was departing, I sat my ass down on the cold floor to help cool myself down. Yes, that's right, I pulled the back of my skirt away so I could sit my ass on the actual floor while I opened my laptop to get on Skype with the new mentor I was about to invest $15,000 into working with.

The money was coming from some corporate contract work I'd done but hadn't been paid for yet, so I placed a deposit to work with her from January and got on the plane to Chile. It was the largest amount of money I'd ever invested in myself in one go. Two and a half years later, I chose to invest $60,000 in another mentor via text message. No phone call. Not even a voice note. That takes self-trust.

I invested well over $250,000 in my personal development and business education between the ages of twenty-five and thirty. I could have purchased many other things with that money but I knew that I was my most valuable asset (and so are you).

You need a huge amount of self-trust to be able to invest large sums of money in yourself. Higher education costs are comparatively large in the United States compared to other countries in the world. Investing over $100,000 into a university education is fairly normal.

That kind of investment is different from the money I spent; you don't need self-trust to shell out large amounts of money for a degree, because you're borrowing trust from the higher education system and your chosen school's brand. You're probably also borrowing trust from the fact that your friends or family made a similar decision to spend large sums on their higher education too.

The kind of self-trust that allows you to invest a quarter of a million dollars into non-formal education before the age of thirty is, I believe, the kind of self-trust that leads to successful entrepreneurship. Self-trust isn't about reckless decision-making or taking on too much risk. It's about confidently making a decision knowing you are backing yourself one hundred percent. It's knowing that when you invest $10,000 in education or mentorship – a very non-tangible thing – you trust yourself to do what it takes to generate ten times that value back.

That's not to say that I commit to creating exactly $100,000 back in value from the investment. I wouldn't want to limit the result in that way. Instead, I've generated value from those investments by partnering with other people inside that program, by creating a collaborative relationship with the mentor, by getting invites to experiences I would never have otherwise received, by creating incredible friendships and by signing clients from within the container.

This requires you to take a huge personal responsibility for yourself and your decisions. You simply cannot play into any kind of victimhood thinking if you want to generate results in your business.

I don't invest in mentorship because I believe the answers are outside of me. And I don't invest in mentorship to perfectly follow that person's proven step-by-step process to achieving a specific result. Their proven process may be a game-changer for you, but implementing it to create a result is not where the true value is in working with a mentor.

I pay to access that mentor's way of thinking. I choose to work with mentors who have created the kind of success and life I desire. I know it's their thinking and perspective that has helped them create their success, so if I can access their thinking and mental models of the world, I can spot my own thinking gaps and close them faster, which will catapult my success. That doesn't mean you need to agree with everything your mentors think and say, but it does allow you to spot your own blind spots.

Question: Hang on, what do you mean by self-trust and how can I build mine?

You can't make great decisions for yourself – and stick to them – without trusting yourself to make great decisions in the first place. Self-trust is your ability to be brave or confident without being reckless or thoughtless. You have an internal compass, and following yours is always the best path to your version of happiness and success.

Yet you might be conditioned to second-guess yourself. In a world where you're surrounded by other people's opinions, it's easy to be swayed from your own inner knowing, and your self-confidence can plummet when you feel like you've messed up or experienced a failure despite your best effort.

Learning to trust yourself starts with looking inward. It's not selfish to be your own authority, it's essential for a fulfilling life, and at its very core, trusting yourself means you look after your own needs and safety.

Having deep self-trust is about trusting your desires and your abilities, which means accepting all your desires as safe guidance for what you're truly meant to be or meant to achieve, and trusting yourself to have the capabilities or fill your skills gaps with learning, so you can achieve your desires.

Our self-trust is either created or eroded during childhood. For example, if your parents regularly swooped in to fix your problems, you may feel helpless in the face of challenges or give up when things become difficult. Equally, if you grew up around parents with a victim mentality, you may be conditioned to believe that life's circumstances are out of your control, such as believing that success happens to other people and not you. This can lead you to decide a dream is out of reach before you ever attempt to achieve it.

If you sense your childhood hasn't set you up for strong self-trust later on, the good news is that you can rebuild and strengthen your self-trust as an adult.

This might be the first time you've come across the notion of self-trust, so how do you know if you have strong self-trust? You might already intuitively know but in case you don't, this short Self-Trust assessment will help you determine how strong your self-trust is.

———

EXERCISE: SELF-TRUST ASSESSMENT

Read each of the statements below and rate yourself out of five based on how true each is for you, where five is very true and one is not true at all.

1. If someone listened to my thoughts, they would hear that I am generally kind to myself.
2. I am confident in the choices I make.
3. I rarely if ever second guess my decisions.
4. When I make promises to myself, I almost always keep them.
5. I rarely if ever look to others to help me make decisions for me.
6. I always say No when I want to say No to others.
7. I believe my opinion and preferences matter and I regularly voice them.
8. I genuinely like myself just the way I am.
9. When I feel emotions, I allow them to flow through me rather than stuff them down or push them away.
10. I'm aware of my own intuition and trust it fully.

Total your score out of fifty to see how strong your self-trust is, then look back at your lowest scores to identify your biggest opportunities for growth in your ability to be a safe container for yourself.

———

The idea of being a safe container for yourself might sound a little bizarre. But the reality is, many of us aren't safe containers for ourselves. You might be breaking promises to yourself or allowing your negative self-talk to run the show in your own head.

I remember being horrendously mean to myself, to the point of trying to control my eating so I wouldn't say such mean things about myself when looking in the mirror. In social situations, I would come across as self-conscious because the thoughts running through my head were all about how weirdly I was coming across or how I wasn't being funny or interesting enough.

I've since swapped my Inner Bitch for an Inner Cheerleader and she's cheering me on every day, telling me how much I accept and love myself, even when I screw up despite trying my best.

I think the years of using the Emotional Freedom Technique (EFT) where you repeat the phrase "...I deeply love and accept myself anyway" must have finally rubbed off on me because I'm now a much safer container for myself. My thoughts are kind and generally speaking, I keep my own promises to myself... unless there's chocolate involved!

If your score out of fifty feels low and you're wondering what you can do about it, here are three very simple steps you can take immediately.

1. Do what you say you're going to do - always.

Make a promise to yourself to always keep your commitments, not just because the commitment is important but because your own self-integrity is deeply important to your ability to trust yourself, and make shit hot decisions for yourself in the months and years to come.

Keep your own word and follow through on what you say you're going to do, not just the things you're going to do for others but most importantly the things you're going to do for yourself. You might notice that you're better at this in some areas of your life than others. For me, keeping my commitments related to going to the gym or eating healthily are the hardest, whereas I'll always follow through on any commitments to do with my business, even if I'm a little delayed with implementing.

When you make commitments to yourself and then don't keep them, your subconscious brain learns that you can't trust yourself, because you don't always follow through. And if you can't trust yourself to stick to simple commitments, then trusting yourself to make great decisions for your business and life becomes a whole lot harder.

2. Listen to your own thoughts and edit accordingly.

If you haven't already been inspired to switch your Inner Bitch for an Inner Cheerleader, here is your invitation to do exactly that right now.

It took until my early twenties for me to understand that my inner thoughts weren't actually the truth. They were just a version of what could be true, but were in fact not the actual reality and were not also believed by everyone else around me.

Some call it mindfulness but I like to see it as being a third-party listener to my own thoughts, as if I am a friend who is listening in on my thoughts and is able to question them from a place of love and wanting the best for me. This allows you to catch the negative or fear-based thoughts that fly through your head, often on repeat. You can replace them with far kinder, more positive thoughts.

Given that you have endless versions of your truth available to you to tell yourself, why not choose a version that supports your mental wellbeing, self-belief and inner peace, rather than tearing yourself down from the inside out with just your thoughts – like so many of us do who are harsh and critical of ourselves.

This won't make you lazy or less likely to achieve your goals. Quite the opposite, in fact, because when you lead your life from a place of self-acceptance, self-liking and eventually self-love, it becomes ten times easier to create forward momentum towards what you want. You're no longer aiming to achieve goals to prove you are worthy, because you know you are already worthy and enough.

Adopt a gentle, nurturing lens for your own thoughts and watch your self-trust and sense of peace skyrocket.

3. Allow yourself time and space to process your own emotions.

Do you push your emotions to the side or numb yourself out so you don't really feel "the moment"?

If so, you're not alone. For ten days after walking out of the McKinsey office for the last time, I didn't feel anything emotionally. I had numbed myself out by preventing myself from feeling any emotions. It was a protective mechanism I'd unconsciously learnt to help me get through the day.

I had to retrain myself to feel and not just bypass my emotions. So how can you do the same if you're not so great at feeling your emotions? I discovered a simple process that got me back in tune with myself and will help you do the same. Even if you're great at allowing yourself to feel emotion, this fourteen-day exercise will tune you in even deeper and increase your levels of happiness in a short period of time.

EXERCISE

This simple, daily check-in process starts with you asking yourself: "How am I feeling out of ten today?"

At the top end of the spectrum, ten is happiness, contentment and joy, while one is high stress or depression.

One to three is the danger zone, four to seven is in the middle, and if you're in the eight to ten zone, you're in a good place.

Rate yourself now to check in with how you're feeling. And then ask what it would take to move your score up by one point. What do you need right now for that to happen?

Do this process daily for at least two weeks and notice the shifts in your self-awareness. Your average score will naturally increase over time.

I took myself from an average of a four to a seven in less than two months and learnt how to really tune into how I felt, rather than gaslighting my own emotions and putting them to the side.

I believe you never truly live life until you give yourself permission to deeply feel. When it comes to making shit hot decisions, you must be able to feel your way through situations, so you can decide from a place of deeply knowing yourself and being able to tap into your felt sense or intuition.

That's not to say that emotional decisions are the best decisions, but feeling your emotions as a data point in your decision-making process is important.

Your self-trust may have been eroded by feeling like you've failed in some way. For example, one of my clients had gone through multiple virtual assistants on her team. Each assistant would only work out for a short few months before the relationship turned sour in some way. This experience led her to decide that she was no good at hiring the right people and couldn't trust herself to make a good decision about hiring team members. She was worried about being let down again.

Another client in a similar situation had unconsciously externalised her lack of self-trust and convinced herself that it wasn't her decision-making or own self-trust in her decision-making that was the problem, but instead had begun to tell herself stories like "it's really hard to find good team members... and therefore I won't try again", or "therefore I am doomed to have a team I need to micromanage forever".

It's easy to make one bad situation or perceived failure mean unhelpful things about you and your ability to make good decisions, which erodes your self-trust and can stop you from making decisions related to that experience again. Consider the times in which you feel like you made a good decision at the time, but it didn't turn out the way you wanted and you were left feeling disappointed or even that you had failed in some way.

I want you to recognise first that you chose to tell yourself a story about that situation and that there are many, many different stories you could tell yourself about that situation. Some stories would be helpful to you and some would not.

You could make that situation mean something positive, such as the way in which you bravely chose to do something that was intimidating at the time, and that you learnt many valuable lessons along the way, which you can now use moving forward to make your next even better. Or you could berate yourself for not knowing better, for being foolish or naive and making a mistake that's really damaged your chances of success in the future.

Our brains are meaning-making machines. Your brain will take any given situation and make it mean something based on your past experiences and the way you choose to see the world, whether consciously or unconsciously.

Question: Will your approach work for me and my niche?

Truth be told, I can't tell you for certain until I've spoken to you. If you'd love to have that conversation, I invite you to pop an application in.

You can do that by heading to go.roseradford.com/apply

Once you have shared your details with me and the team, we review your information and will accept you into the next stage if it seems like it could be a good fit. We have a limited number of spots available to work together so if it's not a good fit, you can trust that I'll let you know and refer you to something else if I feel you're better served elsewhere.

You have nothing to lose by popping an application in.

FREE RESOURCES

Do you like super valuable free stuff? Great! Here's how you can grab an insane bundle of digital resources to help you grow your business on evergreen – completely *free*.

The Inside Scoop on My Million-Dollar Evergreen Funnel

Inside this instant-access digital bundle, you'll receive:

- Our high-converting landing pages and an explanation of why they convert far above industry standard, including plug-and-play templates you can use right away.
- The two emails that generate the most applications to work with us in the entire funnel.
- Guidance on the simplest tech set-up that costs less than $150 a month.

- The three game-changing tweaks we made to our Facebook Ads to 10x our conversion rate and overall profit.
- Your own profit calculator for your evergreen funnel.

Download the bundle here: www.million-dollar-funnel.com

BIBLIOGRAPHY

BOOKS

Menendez, A. (2019). *The Likeability Trap: How to Break Free and Succeed as You Are.* New York: HarperCollins.

ONLINE RESOURCES

Zoltners, A.A., Sinha, P., & Lorimer, S.E. (2020). *Why Women Are the Future of B2B Sales.* Harvard Business Review.

Zetlin, M. (2018). *Women Entrepreneurs Earn 28% Less Than Men. Here's Why.* Inc.

Pew Research Center (2023). *Gender Pay Gap Facts.* Pew Research Center.

Xactly (2019). *State of Gender Equality in Sales Report.* Xactly Corporation.